Emotional Intelligence and Cognitive Behavioral Therapy (CBT) (2 Books in 1)

Reduce Your Anxiety While Increasing Your IQ, Self-Awareness and Mastery of Relationships Using CBT

By: Daniel Patterson

Emotional Intelligence,

One Book Packed with Easy Ways to Improve Your Self-Awareness, Take Control of Your Emotions, Enhance Your Relationships and Guarantee EQ Mastery

By: Daniel Patterson

Table of Contents

Introduction
    Chapter 1: Understanding Emotional Intelligence
    Chapter 2: Emotional Intelligence Test
    Chapter 3: Getting Started
    Chapter 4: Become More Self-Aware
    Chapter 5: Discover Your Passion
    Chapter 6: Express Yourself
    Chapter 7: Manage Your Relationships
    Chapter 8: Manage Yourself
    Chapter 9: EQ at Work
    Chapter 10: Improve Your Leadership Skills
    Chapter 11: Mistakes to Avoid
Conclusion

Introduction

Congratulations on downloading *Emotional Intelligence: One Book Packed with Easy Ways to Improve Your Self-Awareness, Take Control of Your Emotions, Enhance Your Relationships and Guarantee EQ Mastery* and thank you for doing so. Whether you are familiar with the concept or not, rest assured that emotional intelligence is affecting your everyday life in a variety of ways. What's more, even if you haven't heard the term before, you can bet any potential employers out there that you are interested in have, which means remaining in the dark could very well cost you the job of your dreams somewhere down the road.

This is why the following chapters will discuss everything you need to know regarding emotional intelligence, what it is and how you can ensure you have as much of it as possible. You will learn all about the basics of emotional intelligence, test your current level of emotional intelligence, and learn how to get started improving your weaker areas. You will then learn about becoming more self-aware, finding your inner passion and expressing yourself more fully.

This will then lead you to improve the way you manage relationships with others as well as yourself. You will then learn how it can improve your workplace and how having a high level of emotional intelligence can make you a better leader. Finally, you will find a variety of common mistakes that many people make when trying to improve their emotional intelligence as well as what you can do to avoid them.

There are plenty of books on this subject on the market, thanks again for choosing this one! Every effort was made to ensure it is full of as much useful information as possible, please enjoy!

Chapter 1: Understanding Emotional Intelligence

While it is rarely discussed as frequently as traditional intelligence, emotional intelligence (EQ) is just as important, if not more so, in the average person's day to day life. It is responsible for turning thoughts into actions, creating new connections between individuals and generally ensures you make the right decisions when it matters most. Broadly speaking, it can be seen as the ease with which a person can access their emotions to identify, manage, and understand a wide variety of scenarios including those that involve making an empathetic connection to others, lower stress or communicate effectively. It is also a vital part of understanding body language and nonverbal cues which can be useful in both business and social circles.

While generally spoken of as a single concept, emotional intelligence is actually a combination of three separate skills. The first of these is emotional awareness which can be thought of as the ability to understand what other people are feeling. This goes hand in hand with the skill of understanding and managing your own emotions. They both make it possible to nurture the ability to use one's own emotions or the emotions of other for specific goals. While these all might seem like very straightforward skills when written as a list, the fact of the matter is that those with high emotional intelligence across the board are quite rare.

When it comes to self-improvement, there are few things more universally beneficial than taking the time to improve your emotional intelligence. Intelligence will get you an interview, or maybe a first date, emotional intelligence will ensure that everything goes according to plan. If you are unsure what your current level of emotional intelligence, consider how confident you are of your performance in the following areas:

In the workplace: The complex social interactions that the workplace requires can be complicated to see clearly at the best of times and if you have a low emotional intelligence level then you are likely constantly baffled by why those around sometimes walk on egg shells around certain individuals. Improving your emotional intelligence level will instead allow you to excel, motivate others and eventually put you in line for a leadership position. In fact, emotional intelligence is now routinely considered part of the screening process for many management positions.

Your general health: Emotional intelligence allows you to understand your own emotions more thoroughly which in turn makes it easier to manage them effectively. This, in turn, should make it easier for you to manage your stress levels which ultimately leads to a lower risk of cardiovascular disease, infertility, stroke, blood pressure and a general weakening of the immune system. This doesn't just include your physical health, but also your mental well-being. If left untreated, high stress levels can also lead to anxiety, depression and other potentially serious mental issues. A failure to connect with others can also lead to long term feelings of isolation which can even lead to suicidal thoughts.

Interactions with others: The better you come to understand your emotions the more likely you are to understand what other people are feeling which in turn makes your interpersonal relations proceed much more smoothly. The relationships formed as a result of a high emotional intelligence also allow for more mutually beneficial relationships to form.

Productivity: Emotional intelligence has a high correlation with an individual's work performance. Research has revealed that emotional intelligence is twice as crucial as technical/cognitive abilities even among professions such as engineering. Emotionally intelligent managers, supervisors, and leaders are way more effective in managing teams, motivating people and negotiating.

They create a more positive atmosphere with happier workers, who are an asset to any organization. Happier workers translate into higher morale, low absenteeism, reduced attrition rate, and higher productivity. This leads to happier customers, more sales and higher profits. Thus emotional intelligence is an invaluable trait when it comes to success in the workplace. Whilst everyone within an organization possesses more or less the same technical competency and educational qualifications, only a few rise up the corporate ladder because of their ability to manage people and their emotions.

An emotionally intelligent leader who understands the true value of identifying and managing emotions can empower his/her subordinates with these skills on a daily basis. Discipline or self-regulation is essential when it comes to keeping your emotions in check, avoiding panic, remaining calm and being an asset to the team. Emotionally intelligent folks have little trouble in recognizing and managing potentially destructive emotions that can create stress and lower productivity. The approach is calmer, more confident and efficient. Rather than experiencing a more touchy view, these folks depend on their ability to possess a more realistic view of themselves and others.

Coping With Life Challenges: Don't you sometimes look at some people and wonder how they are able to stay afloat through the most challenging situations and emerge even more successful than before? Chances are, these guys score high on emotional intelligence. Emotionally intelligent folks have the ability to calm their body and mind to view things from a clearer and more objective perspective. Their acts are more mindful and less panic struck.

Greater calmness, objectivity and clarity award you more resilience where life's challenges are concerned. Emotional intelligence equips you with those skills to take on the toughest challenges life throws at you with resilience.

Early days

First discussed academically in the 1960s, the importance of emotional intelligence wasn't fully grasped until the 1990s thanks to a pair of researchers named Peter Salovery and John Mayer. In their whitepaper titled *Emotional Intelligence*, they discussed the idea that EQ and IQ were of equal importance with many people finding EQ more useful in their day to day lives. More importantly, they also showed how EQ can be measured in much the way that IQ can.

They also put forward the idea that EQ has four different aspects perceiving emotions, using emotions, understanding emotions and managing emotions. Maye and Salovey even went so far as to explain that EQ is more than simple cognitive ability which means it can easily be applied to IQ as well. Daniel Goldman followed up on the initial research with a book titled *Emotional Intelligence: Why It Can Matter More Than IQ* which was released in 1995 where it would remain on the bestseller list for more than a year and a half before going on to be published in more than 40 different languages. It provided much the same information as the Mayer and Salovey paper but was packaged in a way that people could relate to their everyday lives.

Important elements of emotional intelligence

While there are many different theories surrounding emotional intelligence, there are a few basics facets that everyone can agree on which include things like self-awareness, self-regulation, motivation, and empathy, each of which are discussed in detail below.

Self-awareness: Self-awareness can be thought of as one's ability to recognize person emotions, internal states, preferences, resources, and even intuition. It is the entry way for many people when it comes to improving their emotional intelligence as becoming more in touch with yourself is a great way to start naturally improving your EQ as well. This is thanks to the fact that understanding your own emotions in an indepth way is the first step to effectively managing them in the longterm. Being more aware of your own thoughts and their effect on your actions also makes it easier to empathize with others as well.

Self-regulation: Self-regulation is a direct response to increased self-awareness as a person needs to be in-sync with their emotions as well as their causes and effects before they can be effectively regulated. Thinking prior to acting is vital when it comes to controlling your emotions as it will also make it easier to withhold judgement of those around you as well. As a general rule, the more intense a situation is the more likely people are to react in an emotional way, including taking something personally or overreacting to criticism. Self-regulation can also make it easier to put yourself in another person's shoes which is a great way to increase the odds of a positive emotional response rather than a gut reaction.

Motivation: Emotional intelligence and laziness are natural enemies as those with high emotional intelligence are naturally driven to reach their goals, regardless of what the specifics might entail. Having an increased level of motivation is beneficial in virtually every facet of life and is the perfect way to give yourself the extra push you need to get yourself out of the rut you have been stuck in.

Empathy: Empathy plays a large role in your day to day interactions with those around you. While many people often confuse it with either sympathy or compassion, empathy is a person's ability to relate to and understand the emotions of those around them. It is directly related to withholding judgement which is an aspect of self-regulation. People with a high level of empathy find they can easily understand when other people are feeling a specific way and understand to respond in such a way that it meets their goals and desires.

As an example, if you had a friend who was depressed because they didn't get the raise they were hoping for, if you were an empath you would naturally feel the need to try and cheer that person up by redirecting them away from their depressed state, even if you personally don't much care about their situation one way or the other. Empathy can be thought of like the difference between listening to what another person has to say and understanding the feelings they are likely having as a result.

Social skills: Those who are able to cultivate naturally high EQ often become leaders of one sort or another simply because they have a natural ability to connect with others, be inspiring and manage their emotions as needed. This is often a culmination of the various elements of emotional intelligence working in tandem and some leaders may do these things without fully being aware of what exactly it is they are up to, it is just the result of their natural abilities manifesting themselves.

IQ vs. EQ

If you hope to improve your emotional intelligence then it is important you understand where the line exists between EQ and IQ (Intelligence Quotient). IQ is based on a number of standardized tests that work together as a means of measuring a person's intellectual and academic ability and intelligence. EQ, on the other hand, can be measured via tests but is often best gauged by watching how a person interacts with others.

A person is born with a fixed IQ that is unlikely to move much, for most people, during their lifetime. EQ, on the other hand, is partially a result of innate ability but is largely developed based on the experiences a person has throughout their formative years. IQ can be thought of as a group of parameters that serve to dictate the likely extent of a person's cognitive abilities while EQ serves as a foundation that a person is allowed to build on based on the experiences they have in life. What it boils down to, essentially, is the difference between cognition and intuition. EQ is how IQ is often best put to use. To put it another way, IQ is what you can do and EQ is why you would want to do it.

While IQ was long considered the standard when it came to measuring someone's overall likelihood for success for more than 100 years, for the past 20 years or so EQ has been on the rise when it comes to the metric that companies look to first in prospective employees. This is a natural evolution as while an IQ test can go a long way towards determining a child's ability in the classroom, it will do little to show how that child will learn most easily, how they will interact with other children or if they are able to think critically in high pressure situations.

This is why many major industries have shifted away from IQ tests in favor of EQ assessments that tell them more useful information about their future employees. While this isn't necessarily surprising, what is surprising is the results. One study from 2016 found that 71 percent of the hiring managers interviewed said they valued EQ over IQ and 60 percent they would no longer hire a person with high IQ and low EQ, regardless of the circumstances.

Understanding emotion

A basic part of emotional intelligence is the ability to easily identify the emotions that you or another person are experiencing in order to ensure you are always in control of your emotions rather than having it the other way around. The best way to get started down this path is to understand the primary human emotions and their distinguishing characteristics.

It is generally believed that there are six primary emotions that have been hardwired into the human brain over the years until they are virtually the same for everyone on the planet. What's more, these emotions also illicit the most instinctual and all around strongest responses out of all the emotions a person can feel. These are anger, disgust, fear, happiness, sadness, and surprise. These can essentially be considered the building blocks upon which all other emotions are based.

Emotional components: Mayer posited that an emotion is formed when a variety of cognitive, experimental and biological states all occur at the same time. Thus, a basic emotion needs three primary aspects, starting with subjective/cognitive experience which relates to the specific emotion you are feeling. Next is the physiological response which relates to the way in which the emotion manifests within you. Finally, there is the behavioral response which is how you express the emotion to the world.

While the basic aspects of the core emotions are going to be the same across the board, much of the rest of the experience is bound to be subjective based on things like culture, race, and age as well as a variety of other classifiers. Furthermore, it is also important to think about the many ways in which a particular person could express a specific emotion in its purest form as opposed to when it is mixed with other emotions or aspects of their life. Some of the potential responses are outlined here:

Psychological response: The Cannon-Bard Theory of emotion posits that people experience emotion, along with the physical aspects of those emotions, at the same time. Thus, if your hands are sweating and you feel nervous then it can be difficult which caused the other. This is based on the way the sympathetic nervous system works. It is a subsystem of the autonomic system which controls a variety of involuntary functions like breathing. This system is also responsible for the flight or fight response as well as the physical responses that come along with all emotions. Meanwhile, the amygdala also plays a part in the physical response related to some emotions as well as feelings of thirst and hunger.

Behavioral response: The behavioral response aspect of an emotion is the way that an emotion is expressed, separated from the physical response it generates in the first place which includes things ling frowning, smiling and other expressions related to emotions. While some of these are sure to be universal, others will require more EQ to break down, especially if you are trying to figure out an emotion someone else had when there are cultural differences to consider. With enough practice, you will be able to determine what the other person's emotional response to a specific situation is going to be. When another person expresses an emotion, someone with a high EQ will be able to do more than just identify it, they will be able to respond and interpret tit based on the body language and expression that are being used.

Chapter 2: Emotional Intelligence Test

In order to actually get started improving your emotional intelligence, it is important to understand where you are starting out from. Answer the following list of questions honestly and remember if you lie then the only person you are going to end up hurting is yourself. Once you have tallied up your answers, keeping reading for a breakdown of just what your score means.

When going over the following questions, it is important to be as honest with yourself as possible. There are no right answers here, just the most accurate answers for your specific scenario. Only by answering honestly will you be able to determine a baseline that you can successfully work from in the future.

100 percent false *responses are worth 1 point*
Mostly false *responses are worth 2 points*
Slightly true *responses are worth 3 points*
Mostly true *responses are worth 4 points*
100 percent true *responses are worth 5 points*

1. When I am experiencing an emotion I can typically identify it
100 percent false
Mostly false
Slightly true
Mostly true
100 percent true

2. I can remain calm regardless of the situation
100 percent false
Mostly false
Slightly true
Mostly true
100 percent true

3. Other people would say I am a good listener
100 percent false
Mostly false
Slightly true
Mostly true
100 percent true

4. When I am anxious or upset I can calm myself down quickly
100 percent false
Mostly false
Slightly true
Mostly true
100 percent true

5. Working in large groups is easy for me
100 percent false
Mostly false
Slightly true
Mostly true
100 percent true

6. Focusing on long-term goals is easy for me
100 percent false
Mostly false
Slightly true
Mostly true
100 percent true

7. Negative feelings and thoughts don't stick with me
100 percent false
Mostly false
Slightly true
Mostly true

100 percent true
8. I understand my strengths and weaknesses
100 percent false
Mostly false
Slightly true
Mostly true
100 percent true
9. Negotiation and defusing conflict come easily to me
100 percent false
Mostly false
Slightly true
Mostly true
100 percent true
10. More often than not I enjoy working
100 percent false
Mostly false
Slightly true
Mostly true
100 percent true
11. I look forward to constructive feedback
100 percent false
Mostly false
Slightly true
Mostly true
100 percent true
12. When I set a long-term goal the timeline is often accurate
100 percent false
Mostly false
Slightly true
Mostly true
100 percent true
13. The nonverbal cues of others are often clear to me

100 percent false
Mostly false
Slightly true
Mostly true
100 percent true

14. I find it easy to make small talk

100 percent false
Mostly false
Slightly true
Mostly true
100 percent true

15. Listening accurately is something I am good at

100 percent false
Mostly false
Slightly true
Mostly true
100 percent true

Understanding your score

Now that you have answered all of the questions, it is time to add up your score. Remember, 100 percent false statements are 1 point, Largely false statements are worth 2 points, Slightly true statements are worth 3 points, Mostly true statements are worth 4 points and 100 percent true statements are worth 5 points.

A score of 15 to 34: If you scored between 15 and 34 on the EQ test, then you have certainly come to the right place. You are in this category if you frequently feel quite overwhelmed in situations that are stressful or emotionally taxing. You also fall into this category if you routinely avoid conflict or it stresses you out beyond your ability to handle it. This category also includes those who have a difficult time calming themselves once they do become frustrated or upset.

If you achieved a score in this range it is important to start working on improving your EQ as quickly as possible. Nevertheless, it is also important to understand that it will be an uphill journey but one that will eventually become easier. It is by no means insurmountable, however, and as long as you persevere you should begin seeing real results sooner than you might ultimately think.

A score of 35 to 55: If you score in this range, then you have a mild to moderate (depending on precise score) level of EQ already. This means that you are likely able to get along with other people who are already affable but may have trouble in more advanced EQ scenarios. If you are in this category, then it is important that you stay the course and remain aware of where your specific strengths and weaknesses lie. While you won't be learning and improving every day, you still have plenty to learn as long as you continue to seek it out.

A score of 56 to 75: Congratulations, if you scored in this general range then most people likely consider you to be quite charming, regardless of whether or not they vocalize it. You are likely someone that people come to for advice and, odds are, your opinion generally carries a lot of weight in your social circles. Even still, there is likely more you can do and no one ever accomplished anything by sitting on their laurels which means you should still be looking for new ways to improve. One great way of doing so is by taking on a leadership role at work. When doing so, it is important to take care that you don't overextend yourself in an effort to make others happy.

Chapter 3: Getting Started

After you have a good understanding of what emotional intelligence is all about, as well as the myriad of things that it can do for you and where your EQ is currently at, the next thing you are going to want to do is to get yourself used to the idea of improving in this fashion through some small starter exercises. Especially if your EQ is much lower than you would like, it is important to keep in mind that you won't be raising it to the mid-70s overnight which means it is best to start off with some simple practice to get into the swing of things.

First things first, you are going to want to practice the following at least twice a day, once in the morning and once at night to keep you in an emotionally intelligent mindset. When choosing the time to start your exercises, ensure that it is a time you can easily repeat each day as your mind will take to the practice more easily with the added repetition. Finally, you will want to practice each and every day for a full month in order to ensure these exercises become full-blown habits.

Learn to better understand your feelings: If you are like most people, then your days are a hectic mess of deadlines and appoints that make it difficult to find the time sit and collect your thoughts, much less assess your emotional state. This problem is often compounded as a stressed and distracted mindset is often going to be enough to let poorly thought out actions slip through which will rarely do anything that is going to improve the situation. This is why it is so important to always practice communicating when you get a chance to ensure you will be able to prioritize communications with others when they do occur.

Emotions are frequently tied to events that are taking place in your immediate vicinity, but that doesn't mean that the emotions you are feeling are automatically going to be a valid response to the events in question. In fact, the emotion you are feeling in the moment could easily be tied to something that the current situation is only bringing to mind. If you find yourself in this type of situation, then regardless of how the emotion feels to you, it is still an incorrect response and you need to work on breaking the association in question. Learning to understand which emotions you are feeling in the moment, and why, is a crucial step to improving your EQ in the long-term.

Being aware of your feelings is a skill which means that it can be improved if you are willing to practice doing so. To that end, you should pick a set time each day to practice this skill, once in the morning and then again in the evening. When practicing, you are going to want to check in with all of the emotions you have felt since your last check in and determine if the emotion you felt was an accurate response to the stimuli that was taking place at the time.

One of the hardest things about emotional intelligence is learning how to express your emotions. This isn't about having emotions; even those with higher emotional intelligence will experience emotions. But it is about taking a step back and realizing which emotions fit into a situation and which ones shouldn't be allowed.

Look more closely at your emotions: Once you have gotten more comfortable being aware of your mental state, the next step is to get into the habit of being more aware of the way your actions are being directly effected by your emotions and which actions are most frequently tied to which emotions. It is important to consider both the positive and negative emotions you are feeling as this information is worthwhile for all emotions, not just those you are looking to get rid of.

In fact, the more you learn about the emotional spectrum as a whole, the easier you will find identifying the emotions that others are feeling as well. What's more, after you have catalogued a wide variety of emotions for reference you will be able to understand when you are heading down a bad emotional road so you can detour as needed. When looking into the behaviors your emotions lead you to most frequently, it is vital that you don't make the process more difficult than it needs to be by passing judgement on the things you are feeling.

Passing judgement in this way is only going to add even more complex emotions on top of everything else that is already going on which will make it more difficult to get to the bottom of things than it would otherwise be. Rather than judging yourself, you should find it far more beneficial to make a real effort to be aware of the feelings you are having and the actions they cause as you feel them both in the short and long-term. You will also want to watch the way they affect your ability to communicate, your overall feeling of personal satisfaction and your person productivity.

Expressing your emotions: Managing the way that you react to your emotions means that you are able to choose how and when you express any emotion that you are feeling. Those who are able to manage their emotions understand that it is healthy for them to express their feelings, but that there are a right time and place for expressing these. These individuals understand the following:

- They know that they are able to choose their reactions rather than allowing the emotions to be in charge. This can help them from doing or saying things that they will regret later on.
- They know when it is best to speak out, and when it is better for them to hold back.
- They understand that whatever reaction they have will influence what will happen next, such as how they feel or how others will respond to them.

Understand you are responsible for your actions: If your EQ is on the lower end of the spectrum then it may be hard for you to understand that you are responsible for all of your emotions, even when this doesn't feel as though it is the case. The fact of the matter is that even if it doesn't feel like it, each emotion is a response to external stimuli and that response is a choice. With enough practice, you will find that you can take responsibility for your feelings and the actions that these feelings may have ultimately caused.

What this means is that you may find it helpful to start each day while you are working to improve your emotional intelligence by setting aside a few minutes to think about this fact and what it means to you in both the short and the long-term. You may even find additional success by treating it as your own personal mantra so that you are thinking it about it each and every day. Eventually, it should be such a common part of your thought process that you will come to think of your emotions as a tool as opposed to an unknown variable that needs to be guarded against. When it comes to working to improve your EQ once and for all, this is a vital step to work towards.

Respond properly: When it comes to dealing with situations that are emotionally charged, the most common way that many people tend to react is by doing the first thing that comes to mind, without consciously thinking anything through. Reacting in this way is a type of unconscious, automatic response which is why it is such a natural part of your average snap judgement. With practice, however, you will find that responding to a situation as opposed to reacting to it will make it much easier for you to make well-reasoned and rational decisions which will lead to more effective responses overall. While reacting without thinking is an easy way to let off some emotional steam, the results are rarely going to turn out in your favor, especially when compared to the way things could have worked out if you took the time to respond in the best possible way instead.

To help you get into the habit of responding to a situation instead of reacting to it, it is important to get into the habit of taking a few extra moments to center yourself when you experience an emotionally charged situation. This will also give you some extra time to make sure that what you are doing is really responding as opposed to reacting in a slightly delayed fashion. The best way to go about doing so is to think about why it is you feel the way you do prior to making this choice. You will also want to think about the choice you are making and consider if it is really the best way to resolve the situation that is taking place in a way that is the best for everyone. Putting yourself in the other party's shoes will also make it easier to empathize with them, especially at first.

Keep track of your values: As you go about your day it is crucial that you consciously monitor the things you do and consider why it is you are doing them. While doing so it is important to take the time to consider if it is really the best thing you can be doing with your time right now. If you come to the realization that you are in error, don't bother making yourself feel bad about it and instead look deeper into yourself and determine what you need to be doing to see the best possible results.

One useful exercise at this juncture is to make a list of everything that you do in a given day as a means of helping you identify those things that are actually the most important to you. This should, in turn, help you to more easily pinpoint the drains on your time so you know what to cut out in order to more easily reach your goals. This will also allow you to more easily focus on the feelings you are experiencing, ultimately allowing you to know yourself more thoroughly that would elsewise be the case.

If you find out that you are doing things for the wrong reasons, your best bet is to look at your core values as there is a good chance that something somewhere is out of whack. If you look closely at it you should be able to find something that has changed that is the cause. With so much information at your fingertips, you should easily be able to find a way to work through whatever it is that is giving you pause. Look at what has changed in your life lately that may have altered your emotions in such a way that you would not have approved of.

If you find this happening to you, it is important to do what you can to avoid getting discouraged if you can't quite connect the cause to the effect as it can be difficult to sometimes get to the heart of the matter without digging even deeper. With enough dedication and hard work, however, you should be able to find what it going on and what changes you will ultimately need to make in order to ensure things ultimately get back on track.

Hold yourself accountable: No one is going to force you to better yourself. You have to make yourself do it. Self accountability is the hardest thing that a person can do, and it is also one of the best gifts you can give yourself. It is a self-discipline in itself because without self accountability, you will not be able to reprimand yourself if your will power slips. No one is going to scold you but you, so you have to hold yourself to a high standard and avoid falling from that

Do you remember being a kid, and when you did something wrong you got in trouble, but when you did something right you got an award? Well, adult life is like that as well, only you are the one who dishes out the penalties and rewards. The trick is not to reward yourself for a poor job, even though it can be tempting. You have to find a system and stick with it.

Having rewards and penalties will give you more of a reason to hold yourself accountable. You want to get the rewards, and it will make it easier to do what you are wanting to do if you have a reward to look forward to. You can reward yourself any time you take a step in the right direction towards your goal, however, make sure that the reward matches the size of the step. If you are on a diet, and you have a weekend long cheat binge after dieting for two days, you are nullifying your progress, making it harder to get anywhere. For small steps, think small rewards. For big steps, think big rewards. Of course, penalties should match the offense as well.

Chapter 4: Become More Self-Aware

Since childhood, most people are taught to categorize and judge their emotions and the emotions of others. What is omitted in this early training is how to be more aware of personal emotions and how they affect decisions, behaviors, and beliefs about oneself and others. For example, you may have learned as a child that crying was bad. Consequently, as an adult, you rarely cry and would never dream of doing so in public. If someone you trusted had taught you that crying was only a way your body allows you to let off some built-up steam and stress, then perhaps you would be more capable of handling your own tears and feel more comfortable around others when they feel the need to cry.

That's the first step in creating more emotional awareness. Let go of your past judgments and categories where you have conveniently tucked away the emotions with which you feel uncomfortable. When you have tears or see someone else tearing up, grab a tissue and experience the waterworks. You'll be surprised at how refreshed you will feel when you let yourself experience the honesty of your emotions without the need to try to explain or rectify the situation. Just feel the raw emotion. As you think about what you are feeling with the tears, most of them will probably just dry up on their own, and you'll be consumed with wonder about the feelings associated with the tears.

The process of awareness is enhanced when you close the door on judgment and criticism. Keep in mind; there's not a right or wrong time to feel your emotions. The only thing that is wrong is deciding not to feel at all. When you allow yourself to feel and think about the emotions you are feeling; you have increased awareness of how to use your feelings to positively impact your life.

Personal assessment

In order to become as self-aware as possible, you will need to rate yourself when it comes to your personal strengths and weaknesses. If you find that you have a difficult time being open and honest with yourself about such things then you may find better success asking others for help instead. You may also find standardized personality tests are useful in helping you pinpoint various personal values, skills, and abilities. Finally, if you just can't seem to get started then the following tips might help.

Try writing things down: In order to be more actively self-aware a good place to start is by writing down your short-term priorities and your long-term plans. You will likely have goals or plans floating around in your mind already, so taking the time to actually write them down can be a great way to ensure you are always on the right track no matter what. Once you get into this habit regularly you should find that it makes your goals seem more concrete which, in turn, should make it that much easier for you to work hard at achieving them.

A good place to start is to make a list of all the things you want to accomplish in the short-term, including any specific goals and plans. This should allow you to decide what to focus on first as well as what metrics you can use in order to gauge your progress along the way. A great example of this is Warren Buffet, who is also known for clearly articulating the reasons he makes a specific investment at the time of the investment as opposed to looking for ways to justify his choices after the fact. He keeps a journal that is full of his investment records that helps him determine if a new investment is a good choice based on the past information he has accumulated.

While your personal journal will likely cover more than just investments, you can still use the same approach to success that Warren Buffet does. Specifically, you can clearly lay out the plans you are going to work on next, be it starting a business, getting a promotion, or simply going on vacation before writing down why exactly it is you want to accomplish these goals. The reasons you come up with should not only be well thought out, but they should also be relevant to your immediate situation as well.

The goal of this exercise is to make it easier for you to think about your plans for the future in an active, as opposed to a passive, way. It is easy to feel frustrated at a time when you are stuck in one place and don't seem to be making headway; keeping this journal should help you ensure that you always feel like you are moving in the right direction. When you write your goals down and can refer to the reasoning behind them when you are feeling dejected, you will find it is far easier to see where your real plans exist and which goals are actually just pipe dreams.

When you come across a pipe dream you will find it is then far easier to change your game plan and try something different in a proactive, positive way. What's more, you will often find that planning ahead will be enough of a boost to cause a significant improvement to your average results as well which means you can look forward to better results most of the time.

When it comes to following through it is vital that you use a physical journal and also that you write in it each and every night. Keeping a running tally of your experiences how they made you feel and the physical reactions that came along with them. Make sure you take note of physical expressions of the emotions including sore shoulders, stiff neck or an increased heart rate. While it may be difficult to keep track of everything that is going on in your head at first, with some practice, you will find that it becomes far easier and that you become more aware of your true inner state on average without even trying.

With this out of the way, the next thing you will want to do is to expand on this list so that it outlines the part you played at each juncture. Listing the role you played in the experience is extremely important if you ever hope to change things for the better and can include things like mother, father, sister, brother, employee, spectator, customer, etc. You will want to keep your roles fairly broad to ensure that you will see some overlap from day to day so that you can start to see patterns emerging.

With enough time, you should find that you are able to use the journal as a roadmap for moving forward in the most productive fashion possible as it will make it much easier to properly associate specific roles with the emotions commonly associated with them. Don't forget, forewarned is forearmed which means that if you do find yourself in a situation with anticipated negative connotations then you will find it much easier to navigate because you have been their before and know what to expect. Ideally, this will give you the extra moment you need to prepare yourself to handle things as effectively as possible.

It is important that you do your best to isolate the specifics regarding each emotion as thoroughly as you can. Part of this should include mental checking off the emotions you are likely to feel in a given situation. Names have power, after all, and naming your emotions is often the first step in successfully taming them once and for all. After you are properly aware of the emotions you are likely to experience in the short-term you should find that it is easier to guard against them. In fact, with enough practice, you will find that your defenses should naturally rise to the occasion without you having to actively think about it.

Ask other people for feedback: While many people naturally feel the urge to go crawl under a rock when the idea of peer feedback comes into play, all feedback is not inherently negative. What's more, feeling that this is the case is only likely to cause you to miss out on valuable opportunities to learn more about your strengths and weaknesses including many you may not be aware of unless someone else pointed it out to you. In fact, the sooner you begin to understand the type of feedback you are dealing with the sooner you will be able to start accepting the help some people are trying to provide you with

There are many ways to start getting in the habit of accepting constructive feedback, starting with simply asking that those closest to you don't hold back on their personal criticisms of your everyday life. If you are the sort of person who fears honesty of all types then this is the place to start as you can trust that these individuals are only going to tell you the types of things you really need to know while at the same time only saying things that sting when they are really necessary.

To get started, the first thing you will need to do is to speak with those who are closest to you and express to them what you are trying to do and how they can help. You will want to ask for their truest, most honest opinions regarding your day to day personal presentation. Before you begin you will also want to do everything in your power to let them know that there will be no consequences for the things they say and they are in a place where they can safely express their opinions. While you are sure to get some negative feedback as a result, it is important to do everything you can in order to move things forward as productively as you can if you ever hope to really improve your EQ.

Don't forget, your goal at this point is to collect as much honest feedback as possible which means you are going to want to avoid responding in most instances unless you have something positive to say in return. After you have a better idea of all the things you need to work on you can then ask this same group of individuals to call your attention to negative activities or habits they see you committing while in public. This is especially effective both with issues that have only recently been called to light as well as those that have been previously exposed but are now cropping up again.

As an example, if you are the type of person who always likes to be at the center of attention then your friends might be able to help you with that by calling you out on this tendency as a means of helping you to get it under control before it really starts getting out of hand. As long as you make it clear to your friends that they are really helping as opposed to being rude you should be able to get them to speak up instead of keeping their mouths shut for fear of hurting their feelings.

After you have started to become used to the idea of getting constructive feedback on a regular basis from those closest to you, the next thing to do is to expand this circle to the workplace as well. Generally speaking, most companies will have some type of useful feedback system in place either through management or Huan resources directly. As long as it proceeds in a respectful, productive fashion it is a great way to determine your professional strengths and weaknesses at a particular point in time so you know where to focus in order to improve.

While hearing so much feedback all at once might be difficult, especially if you previously avoided it as much as possible, it is important to stick with it and understand that it is a crucial part of the overall process of becoming more self-aware and ultimately getting your EQ to where it needs to be. After all, it is quite easy to find yourself stuck in a routine that works for you, more or less, to the point that you don't actively think of what you are doing day to day or how the things you are doing cause other people to view you. Asking for feedback and working to use what you have learned to improve yourself is the first step towards improving your EQ once and for all.

Uncovering negative patterns

Before you can begin making the sorts of positive life changes that you know will really change your life for the better, you need to understand the patterns that you are regularly repeating and how they affect your day-to-day experience. The best way to do this is to practice as pattern recognition is a skill which means that is the only way you will ever find it easier to manage. If you aren't sure how to start, consider the following tips.

Start by seeing the patterns around you: If you find you have a hard time seeing your own personal patterns, instead turn your attention to the world around you and look for the patterns in everything you see. The more patterns you identify the easier will be to identify additional patterns in the future which is why you will eventually be able to start noticing patterns in the people around you as well. Once you are proficient in seeing the patterns in the world at large, identifying your own patterns should seem much more manageable.

Once you have found the correct pattern identifying mindset, you will find that it is easier for you to determine how each of these patterns contributes to the success or failure of the person or thing exhibiting them. Turn this intuition inward and think about your daily trials and tribulations and how your patterns affect them. While it can be difficult to look at your life from an analytical perspective, it is a crucial skill to develop as it is the only way you will ever encounter real change.

If you feel as though you aren't seeing all the patterns that are available to you, don't worry, your ability to spot them will improve with time. Remember, consider the cause and effect of the things you see and the patterns that contribute to them should become more visible. You may find that grouping relevant information together may make otherwise disparate patterns become more visible.

Start looking for patterns to change: Once you have a clear idea of the patterns as they stand, you can start doing your best to determine what should be changed first for the greatest overall result as well as those you want to double down on to ensure they keep happening the way they currently are for as long as possible. Changing personal patterns is easier said than done, however, as it involves changing personal habits as well, some of which may have been in place for an exceedingly long time. Planning is key at this juncture as it will be extremely easy for you to slip up and fall back into your old habits with really even thinking about it.

As an example, imagine that you take on too much work on a regular basis as a way of avoiding deeper human interactions. With this in mind, you could then make a concentrated effort to not work as much on the weekends and force yourself to follow through by working with coworkers to ensure that the work gets done without requiring extra personal sacrifice on your end.

It is extremely important to follow through on altering the first few patterns that you notice for their negative influence as starting and failing to follow through on personal change is an extremely easy pattern to get into all on its own. If you ever hope to make real progress towards the change that you are aiming for then you need to make sure your pattern regarding change is positive rather than negative. Furthermore, you are going to want to keep in mind the fact that it takes more to make a new plan to change deeply ingrained patterns, it also takes commitment, plenty of time and a state of hyper vigilance that will prevent the pattern from showing up again when you least expect it.

Consider your past: If you are looking for patterns in the moment, then this is most likely why you aren't seeing to many of them. It is much easier to see patterns in the rearview with the benefit of hindsight which is always 20/20. Every pattern can be seen in its results, if you find that you do two different things that ultimately lead to the same outcome then it is important you consider both more carefully to determine what patterns are influencing these results. With two points of data, you have everything you need to find additional ones, assuming you take the time to consider both fully beforehand.

Patterns can also be found in the way that current events are influenced by past events and decisions. Finding similarities in these scenarios can also provide you with the data points you need to plot your patterns. Again, it is all about taking the time to notice these patterns and then acting on them accordingly. Finding patterns is meaningless if you don't act on them.

Patterns to avoid: There are many different types of patterns of behavior that can make it much more difficult to achieve the level of emotional intelligence that you would like. If during your internal survey you come across any of the following, it is important to make a plan to alter then as quickly as possible. The desire for instant gratification will make it difficult for you to commit to a course of action that requires a prolonged period of effort up front, making it difficult to ever commit to real change that could lead to empowerment. They say ignorance is bliss but choosing to remain ignorant about important issues will only lead to trouble in the long run. While it is important to remain a certain degree of control on what is going on around you, an all-consuming desire for control in all spectrums of your life will only cause you more harm than good.

You may find a personal pattern that indicates your flight or fight reaction is skewed one way or the other more than it should be, balance is a key to personal empowerment which is why it is so important that you reorient your gut reaction to things. Finally, you may find that you have a pattern of procrastinating until the last moment either because you are afraid of truly succeeding or because you can't find the motivation otherwise. Regardless of the root cause, this pattern needs to be banished completely if you ever hope to find true inner empowerment.

The first step to doing something about a counterproductive pattern is to admit that you are in fact in the midst of a pattern. If you find yourself in the same not exactly ideal situation more than 4 times, then odds are there is a pattern in play. If you find yourself wondering why you never get to do something, why people are always mean or indifferent to you or wondering why some tragedy always seems to befall you then you need to stop asking questions and start working towards change. Once you find you are in a negative cycle you can begin to break it by starting to take steps to initiate change.

Chapter 5: Discover Your Passion

Discovering the things you are truly passionate about is an important part of improving your EQ in the long-term as it will make it possible for you to discover a hidden side to yourself that you previously never new existed. The reason that this is so important is that, for many people, passion is a causality of the digital age. There is so much content out there to consume day in and day out that it is difficult to avoid the idea that there are a million people out there who are better than you at whatever it is you actually like to do with your time. This, in turn, makes the idea of putting off pursuing that passion far easier than giving it your all and trying your best only to end up somewhere in the middle of the pack.

It doesn't take a rocket scientist to see the added stress that comes with striving to reach something you can never achieve, which is never good for anyone but is especially difficult for those who are currently giving it their all to improve their EQ. This chapter will help you to rediscover your passions and also provide you with some tips to help your body and mind slow down somewhat so they don't feel as overworked.

Breathe: The first thing you are going to need to do when it comes to finding your passion is to learn to slow down and breathe once in a while. The easy way to go about doing so is to simply come to terms with the fact that, regardless of how hard you work, you will never be able to please all of the people 100 percent of the time. For those who are naturally driven to help others, the idea of actually saying no can be difficult to the point of making them actually feel sick. The reason it is so difficult is that they can't stand the thought of ever failing anyone, so they put themselves in situations where they sacrifice their happiness and wellbeing for the happiness of others.

If this type of thinking sounds familiar, then it is important to stop thinking of yourself as a martyr and stop before you get hurt. You are only one person, after all, which means that eventually, you will be unable to sustain doing the work of two or more people. Keep in mind that the candle that burns at both ends burns out twice as quickly. If you end up in a situation where you never have the time to think things through, not to mention relax and recharge, you will find that it is much more difficult to improve your emotional intelligence.

While you may find it difficult to take things easy and slow down, especially when you are first getting used to the concept, it is vital that you do what you can in order to ensure it becomes a habit if you want to stand a chance at improving your EQ once and for all. Once you slow down once and for all you will find that it is far easier to find the best version of yourself because you suddenly have the time to start questioning who that is, possibly for the first time in your entire life.

In order to successfully slow down once and for all in the long-term, there are several things you can try. While you will certainly still have some regular tasks that require your attention, you will start to see real results if you can set aside as little as 15 minutes each day to devote to whatever it is you are passionate about. While this might not seem like much, if you give it a try you may be surprised to learn that it makes all the difference in the world. For the best results, you are going to want to set aside time at the same time each day so that it becomes part of your routine come rain or shine. It doesn't matter what you do during this time, it only matters that it is something that you enjoy and something that leaves you feeling happy and relaxed.

While you might find it difficult to disconnect from whatever else is going on during your day at first, it is important to power through as keeping at it is vital to your long-term health in both mind and body and also to help your critical thinking skills remain at their best. When left untreated stress can cloud your judgement and cause you to do things you otherwise wouldn't if you had reacted with a clear head. Thus, the more you can lean to take things down a few notches by relaxing, the easier you will find it to clear your mind and utilize your available EQ like never before.

EMOTIONAL INTELLIGENCE AND COGNITIVE BEHAVIORAL THERAPY

Be unique: While everyone has certain things about them that set them apart from the crowd, many people don't take enough time to focus on the things that make them unique and the ways they can best share their unique talents with the world. This is a far more productive course of action than what they choose to do instead which often amounts to wondering why they don't have the unique talents and abilities of others.

Embracing what makes you unique is a great way to improve both your self-expression and self-awareness while also following your passion which means it is an excellent stop along the path to an improved level of EQ. On the other hand, if you spend all your time questioning why you are not as talented as someone else in one specific way, especially if it is someone you regularly interact with, then this is bound to cause nothing but strife that will make it difficult for you to take additional positive steps moving forward. Letting go of these feelings of envy will not only help you to feel more relaxed but also more able to face what comes next.

Improve your confidence: Building your self-confidence is a dream that many people have but that few people actually follow through on. This is because it can be very difficult to get started if you don't already have plenty of self-confidence, to begin with. Self-confidence is also important when it comes to expressing yourself and your EQ in either the short or the long-term. Even if your self-confidence is in the dumps there are still a number of useful exercises you can do in order to force your mind to see things in a self-confident way.

If you find yourself becoming afraid when it is time to e confident, it is important to understand that the only way to really face this particular fear once and for all is if you master it completely. If you aren't sure about the outcome of a specific event, this uncertainty can easily turn into anticipation which can then turn into fear if you aren't careful. Reacting with anxiety at a time when you should be reacting with self-confidence will destroy any momentum that you may have built up in the interim which means you will end up back at square one.

Thus, you might find that you have a better time being confident in yourself if you react to the anxiety you were feelings as if it were curiosity instead. Rather than being anxious about your outcome, you can then trick your mind into be curious as to the possible outcome instead. Self-confidence and curiosity go hand in hand far more easily than self-confidence and anxiety which means it is as easy way to help you keep up your confidence momentum once it is up and running.

If you find that you always respond to certain situations that require more self-confidence in the same fearful way, it is important to understand just how much the human mind likes patterns. In fact, it loves patterns so much that it will often create them even if they aren't really there. Thus, you might actually be responding to a pattern that is different that the one that currently applies to your give situation. To test this theory, the next time you feel nervous or scared before having to be self-confident, you can take an extra moment to think about what is currently going on and see if your feelings are justified.

Sometimes you will surprise yourself and actually come back with something that warrants a second look; most frequently, however, you will find that there is nothing specific for you to be afraid of which means you can proceed with confidence. If nothing specific comes to mind then the odds are strong that your mind is simply making patterns where none exist. With practice, you should even be able to find that you can improve your self-confidence and then use it to improve your EQ beyond your current levels.

Enjoy yourself: The older you get; the busier life becomes until before you know it all of your time is spent working to pay your bills or preparing for some future point so that even your days off are only ever spent playing catchup. What's more, this type of routine is often quite insidious which means you likely won't realize just how bad things have gotten until you can't even begin to imagine how you ended up buried underneath so many disparate tasks. What's worse, focusing on all of the details without looking at the big picture will do little to improve your EQ, or to help you get out from underneath your mess.

While it might be surprising, the fact of the matter is that simply taking the time to add more fun to your life can be a great way to shake lose your improved mindset and get things moving in the proper direction once more. You will find that it is far more difficult to have a myopic view of life when you have a positive outlook no the things you spend most of your time doing. While it likely doesn't seem like it now, you really can have a home and work life balance.

What this balance is going to be is going to be different for everyone, but even moving in as little as 10 percent in the other direction is sure to have major repercussions on your life. Focusing only on the short-term can make it difficult to ever feel as though you get anything accomplished which can leave you feeling bitter and unfulfilled. When you take the time to really focus on the fun in your life you will be surprised at how quickly even the darkest days seem brighter.

Chapter 6: Express Yourself

If you ever want to improve your EQ, not just in theory but in practice then you will need to do what you can in order to ensure you express yourself as effectively as possible, even when doing so might be more difficult than you would otherwise prefer. Unfortunately, this is often easier said than done as it is often far easier to stay quite and follow the crowd than risk rocking the boat and causing others to think less of you if things don't go according to plan. While this may work for a little while, it is really doing little more than putting a band-aid on the problem and likely making you feel even worse in the interim.

It is important to understand that fully expressing yourself doesn't give you the right to make other people feel worse about themselves unless it is for the greater good or is otherwise unavoidable. Remember, EQ is about more than simply understanding and listening to the feeling of others, it is also all about expressing yourself as clearly as you can when discussing your thoughts, emotions, and feelings. Try and keep the following in mind when it comes to expressing yourself and you will find the process easier than you might expect.

Stand for something: How many times do you meet someone who seems to be lost and confused? They go along with the crowd, doing whatever everyone else wants to do that day and not really giving their own opinion on these things. They may act like they are happy, but usually, they may feel a little resentful because they feel that they can't speak up to others at all. This resentment can really harm them because it will lead to misunderstandings and an attitude of "everyone is against me".

No matter who you are, you need to learn how to stand for something. It doesn't have to be something big. If you are in a group of friends and you don't like Mexican food, make sure to stand up and say that when a group is trying to decide where to eat. It is unlikely that anyone is going to get offended by your announcement; on the contrary, they will take your statement into consideration and you may not have to suffer through an hour at a place that has nothing you want to eat.

That is a small example of standing for something, but it basically means that you need to speak up and make sure that you are heard. A lot of the frustrations that go on in daily life happen because people are too worried about angering others and they will just stay quiet. But when you live your life always worrying about what others think and never getting to do what you want, it can make you stressed and angry and you will likely lose that emotional intelligence because you won't be able to see things from the other point of view.

Of course, your stance should never be cruel and it should take others into consideration. You still need to think about what others like and be empathetic for them, but this doesn't mean that you need to be run over all the time either.

The only person you need to impress is you: While having people respect you certainly beats the alternative, it is important to remember that it is hardly the end of the world if they don't. While this is the opposite of what the digital world teaches, it really is true, the only person you need to worry about impressing is yourself. Regardless of how hard you might work, there are always going to be some people that talk behind your back or get angry when you succeed. If you live your life to the fullest, however, then it is likely to be a small fraction of the whole that you won't need to think twice about which means it is much less of a big deal than it may appear to be at the time.

In order to express yourself to the fullest, the first thing you will want to be aware of is that, regardless of how important or embarrassing something might seem to you at the moment, a vast majority of people will have forgotten about it completely forgotten about it by the next day or, what's even more likely, not even register it in the first place.

It is important to keep this in mind as one of the difficult parts of self-expression that many people fail to master is getting past the thought that other people are going to judge them for expressing themselves in an unguarded way. The truth of the matter is often the complete opposite, most people tend to be so wrapped up in their own personal drama that they won't think twice about anything you say or do, good or bad, which means they will never think anything is nearly as big of a deal as you do.

While the fact that few people are ever going to really give you their undivided attention is somewhat depressing, it is also extremely freeing as it frees you from having to spend all of your time worrying about what other people think. From now on, rather than caring about what everyone around you might say or do you can focus on doing the things you feel good about at the moment and let everyone else take care of themselves.

As long as you feel you can stand behind your words and deed then, regardless of what other people might think, you can move forward with your head held high and nothing to lose. It will also free up some mental space for you to consider how you really feel about a potential action which will make it easier for you to avoid those things that you are sure to regret at some point in the future. Moving forward, make a point of concentrating on impressing yourself first and foremost with everything you do in life and you are bound to end up impressing others in the process.

Locate a muse: If you find yourself having a difficult time expressing yourself from the start, then you may want to find something that can act as a muse to draw the self-expression out of you. While some people are naturally adept at expressing themselves verbally, many people stumble over their words with very little provocation. Luckily, there are plenty of other means of expression which means that if you aren't much of a talker there is likely a better form of expression out there for you.

Thus, the pertinent question becomes what your muse might be and how might you discover it. For some people, this muse will come in the form of public speaking which forces them to interact with strangers while also speaking in front of a crowd of like-minded individuals. Other people might find better success in expressing themselves by writing. While they might not be comfortable speaking in front of a large crowd, this is still a way with words. If you fall into this camp then you may find writing out what you are going to say beforehand to be extremely effective.

For those who feel naturally drawn towards music, playing music can be an excellent way to parse out complicated emotions and playing with a group can be a great way to get used to the idea of being expressive in a social setting. It will also help you get used to the idea of interacting with other people's emotions in the music.

Regardless of what your hobby is there is bound to be something that you can do to help you express yourself more clearly. As long as your hobby allows you to feel free and to stop caring about what others think then you can call that activity your muse. Spending time on anything you truly enjoy will make it easier for you to keep track of your emotions while also letting out your frustration in an inoffensive way that also makes it easier for you to build your EQ.

Chapter 7: Manage Your Relationships

Once you have learned all you can about the emotional tells of those around you, it is now time to learn more about maintaining healthy relationships and expanding new potential interactions. You will also learn to inspire others to action by communicating clearly and diffusing potential conflict. If you hope to successfully manage relationships, then you need to use what you have learned to far in order to determine how you and the other party are affecting one another and what effect external forces are having on the scenario you now find yourself dealing with. Only by having a clear and accurate picture of all the moving pieces will you be able to find the right solution to please everyone.

Determining a true picture of the scenario will then allow you to determine more easily how to proceed based on the tools you have at your disposal. It is important to always get input from everyone involved and to take the time to accurately consider their emotional state in addition to listening to what they have to say. In fact, combining the two data streams would then allow you to get to the bottom of what they are really thinking, regardless of what they might be saying out loud. This way you will be able to work on determining a solution that is right for everyone in an assertive, not an aggressive, fashion.

After you have then come to a decision you will want to add an emotional appeal to your assertive approach to ensure they go along with the solution you proposed because they want to, not because they feel coerced. Making your empathy known is a great way to also make it clear that you are working towards something that will work to everyone's best interested, another surefire way to ensure your assertiveness is taken in the right way. This can be a difficult task at times, but if you have been practicing then you should be up for the challenge.

By recognizing and comprehending emotions, it is possible to manage people. However, there is a very fine line between persuasion and manipulation and trying to alter the emotions of another walks that line. The idea of mind control is a novel one. If only we could be so persuasive that people do what we wanted all the time! Sure that sounds great, but this is not ethical. Manipulating people into feeling guilty or sorry for you is not what this chapter intends. Instead, using emotional intelligence to help interact with people can improve the quality of your life and get you ahead professionally.

The fact that you can understand another person's emotions poises you for a better relationship with that person. Romantic or friendly relationships are a great example. If you can empathize with the wishes of a friend, it can make you a more attentive, meaningful friend in return.

For example, let's say your spouse has had a terrible day at work. You know this because they called you upset and ready to quit. Your remarkable ability to pick up on this anger (it's pretty obvious in this case) helps you decide how to act. You have one of two choices. You can either empathize with them, change your plans and try to make them feel better, or you could be selfish and go out with your friends, leaving your spouse at home to stew with their work problem alone.

Having a good emotional connection and being on the same plane as someone is the key to happy, healthy relationships. Understanding people on a more personal level builds trust and confidence, which shine through in good times and in bad.

Emotional intelligence can assist you in the climb to the top of the corporate ladder as well. Understanding how another person views things can help you persuade them.

Let them share their story: Empathize with people in difficult situations by asking them to share their story or viewpoint about what's happening. Sometimes, you may gain an altogether new perspective (which you hadn't even considered), which will help you understand the person even better. Listen to them intently and non-judgmentally.

Try to get an idea of what they desired and failed to get. Ask them if you unknowingly violated their desires and expectations. Rather than pretending that there's no issue or even worse criticizing/belittling them for acting difficult, try to give them an opportunity to speak and share their feelings. Compassion, empathy, thoughtfulness, and understanding are obvious signs of well-developed emotional intelligence. Obviously, if the negative behavior becomes a habitual pattern, they may need specialized help in the form of counseling for identifying deeper issues.

Notice behavior: This isn't simply about listening to what people are speaking. It goes beyond their speech to pick up both verbal and non-verbal cues like voice tone, body language, gestures, and expressions. Learn to observe people closely to pick up unspoken signs about how they feeling from within.

Take note of their actions by asking yourself questions like – Does the volume of their voice constantly fluctuate? How are their hands placed? Do they turn pink when they speak? Are they maintaining eye contact constantly with you or does their gaze shift frequently? Are they becoming more aggressive and forceful while speaking? Paying attention to these small yet significant signs will offer you plenty of clues about their emotions. This awareness will help you take control of the situation and manage it more efficiently before it goes haywire. It can be a little tough to be both an active participant and observer in a conversation, but it comes with practice.

Take more interest in what's going on around you: The way that you present yourself when talking to others is just as important as the things you say or the topic of conversation. Being truly socially aware means taking the time to go the extra mile and prove to the other person that you value their time and the conversation you are having. You should also think about your most common interactions and how you likely appear to others during them. If you then take the time to put aside any other common distractions while speaking, consider if active listening would improve the situation. If so, take the time to make additional eye contact and really listen to what the other person is saying. Ask yourself if you currently take enough time to gather the input you need from others when it comes to how other people feel about the topics you are discussing.

In addition to keeping all of the above in mind, make it a point to use open body language so it is clear to the other person that you are interested in what they have to say. In order to make other people feel at ease when you are speaking with them, it is vital that you ensure your body language and your spoken language match up as otherwise, the other party will receive conflicting signals that will leave them feeling uncomfortable with your conversation.

Communicating effectively means taking the extra time you need in order to ensure that the messages you are sending, both actively and passively, are not only clear and concise but that they are also received properly by the other party before moving forward. Many people incorrectly feel as though double checking that everyone is on the same page before moving on in a conversation is disrespectful when in reality it shows that you value the other party's time and don't want to waste time later circling back.

Consider their emotional response: Assuming you have already become more familiar with your own emotional responses by this point, it should be a relatively easy jump to adding other people into your thought framework. You should then be able to further extrapolate specifics events, reactions and responses as they are likely to play out so that you are less likely to find yourself surprised when you encounter an unexpected situation. Being able to accurately predict potential situations will also make it easier for you to choose a way to respond that ensures your desired outcome is more likely to occur.

To help a situation along, the first thing you should try is to think about the way in which you would diffuse the emotion at hand if you were dealing with it internally. Taking the time to try and put yourself in the shoes of the other person is an excellent way to get at the heart of their emotion as different people are bound to respond to the same situation in different ways. Rather than shying away from these failures, it is vital to understand that they are a large part of improving your social awareness (and thus your EQ) as there are too many possible emotional variations out there to learn them all simply by studying.

Effectively managing relationships: When it comes to improving your relationship management skills to the point where you can keep your own emotions in control while at the same time effectively managing and directing the emotions of others it is important to understand that the process is a balancing act. To ensure you don't tip things too far in one direction or the other, it is important you have an accurate understanding of how what you say is going to affect the other party, what they are likely to say and how it is likely to affect you and any external forces that might be affecting the situation as well. Only by having a clear understanding of all sides of the situation will you be able to reliably generate a solution that works for everyone.

After you have obtained this type of clear view of the situation you will then find it much easier to come up with the best way to move forward while at the same time successfully keeping all of the many moving pieces in play. While it isn't going to be an instantaneous process right from the start, with practice it will just be something that happens in the background without you having to give it too much active thought.

Once you have determined the best way to move forward given the limitations of the moment, you will then need to consider what you can do in order to ensure the other person comes around to the idea that your plan is the ideal way to move forward in the current juncture. The best place to start is by clearly explaining your desired course of action as well as why you feel it is the best way to move forward effectively. It is also important to make it clear that you are striving to look at things from all possible angles in hopes of coming to a mutually beneficial solution.

When working through these types of scenarios, it is extremely important that you don't make the mistake of trying to juggle too many different emotional states all at once. Start with two and then work you way up from there; if you try and juggle too much from the start you will end up never pleasing anyone. Regardless of the situation, you find yourself in or how many people you are dealing with, your end goal should always remain to be as empathetic as possible to everyone you come into contact with to the point that it is clear you are always just looking to do what's best for everyone involved.

While you should clearly try and lead conversations to your desired outcome, this shouldn't be a blank check to only focus on yourself as this will only lead to the creation of negative relationships in the long-term. If the idea of helping people because it is the right thing to do isn't enough to dissuade you from this course of action then consider the long-term effects of only looking out for yourself, the most relevant of which would be that creating negative relationships limits the number of options you have in the future to the point where you ultimately don't have the tools to succeed.

Keep a social activity journal

Another useful activity when it comes to successfully manage your relationships is to keep a journal of all your social interactions. The goal here is two-fold; first, you will be able to chart your progress which will make it easier to keep the forward momentum going, even when you are in a mental headspace where you don't feel as though you are making any progress. Second, it will help you to keep track of everything that works, and also what doesn't so that you don't need to make the same mistakes twice.

Ask yourself what worked and what didn't: At the end of the day, you should make a list of relevant social interactions you had during the day. While at first, you may not have too many entries, and that's fine, but as you become more outgoing you are going to want to ensure your list is as detailed as possible up until the point where you don't feel you need it any more. After you have made your list, go ahead and outline the broad strokes of the conversation.

While it can be difficult to remember negative interactions, it is important that you go ahead and make it clear exactly what worked about the conversation and what didn't. Once you have done this for a while and have a large enough sample size it will then be easier to pick out patterns in your conversations that you otherwise are unlikely to have noticed. Being consciously aware of these patterns will help you steer towards them, or away from them depending on how effective they ended up being.

Consider your style: Everyone has a conversational style that they are most comfortable with based on their personality. This is something like sarcastic, friendly, flirty, sweet, the specifics don't matter. What matters is that you understand what your strengths are in this situation and play to them, especially when you find yourself in a tough spot that might not otherwise end the way you want it to.

Chapter 8: Manage Yourself

Once you have a clear understanding of yourself and the ways you can jump start the improvement of your emotional intelligence, the first step to actively putting it to use in the real world is applying what you have learned in a real-world context. While you can easily start off having every intention of putting the things you have practiced into action, the stresses and pressures of the real world can make actually following through more difficult than you might expect. In order to ensure that applying your improving EQ becomes a habit, you need to use it every time you come up against emotional stress in any of its forms. Being angry is easy, being the right amount of angry in relation to the situation in question takes far more work but is also far more rewarding in the long run.

Managing the emotions you feel in the moment effectively is all about putting away any victim mentality that you might have and instead enforcing a mentality that allows you to take full control of your emotions as well as the response that form as a result. Before you had taken the time required to properly index and understand your emotions along with their related physical responses, you could be forgiven for thinking the things that you did in the heat of the moment were the result of overpowering emotions, but that is all in the past. If you are strong enough to no longer be caught off guard by your emotions, then you can safely put this mentality away.

Changing your general outlook in terms of what you think about your emotions will ultimately prime you to take charge in the moment when it matters most. Take a moment, right now, to make a commitment to yourself that you will no longer be a slave to your emotions.

Cognitive reframing: If you ever hope to manage the thoughts that are caused by your emotions effectively, you need to be able to manage your thoughts as well. Doing so means being able to interact with your negative thoughts so you can dismiss them, without having to worry about giving in to them in the interim. If you find yourself in a scenario where you feel your negative thoughts rolling in, try the following to determine if they are valid or not.

Consider if the feeling that is welling up is related to a thought or idea that is reasonable or plausible. Oftentimes, especially in negative situations, the human brain likes to extrapolate potential outcomes based on unreasonable information. While the negative response you might have to the emotion is rarely useful, using the emotion as an earmark as to whether the thought is valid can help you cut through exaggerated negative thoughts and emotions.

If, after careful consideration, you find that the situation you find yourself in does, in fact, warrant the feelings you are having, then the next thing you are going to want to do is to find any possible silver lining, no matter how specious it might be. With this done, you will want to focus on that silver lining with as much strength and conviction you can muster. While it may seem like a little thing, this simple change in perspective can be enough to modify your emotions and therefore your thoughts far enough in a positive direction to make a real difference when it comes to seeing results.

Upon closer consideration, you could also end up using the negative situation as a means for self-improvement. When a negative situation arises, rather than letting the negative emotion run its course, a more productive alternative is to instead reframe it with the ultimate goal of personal reflection or self-improvement instead.

If you can't get yourself out of a specific mindset, silly humor might be able to get you there. Silly humor isn't about laughing all your problems away, rather it is a type of cognitive reframing technique that can help cut your anger off at the source. For example, if you find yourself getting angry during rush hour traffic, instead of referring to the other drivers by unflattering derogatory statements, find a silly image and refer to the other drivers by that description instead. If you can make yourself laugh every time you say it, you likely won't remain angry for long.

Being Mindful

Meditation is a skill everyone's heard of but many people really don't understand. In the West, many people often think of meditation as a spiritual or mystical practice, and while it's true that meditation has uses in various religious practices in its most basic form it is a simple thought exercise. Mindfulness meditation teaches the user to focus and occupy the space between their thoughts rather than on those thoughts, understanding their thoughts and the emotions behind them in the process. As you come to recognize these peaceful moments you can use meditation to come back to them. It's a great tool made even more powerful by the fact that it can be done anywhere in any situation. All it takes is practice.

Studies have shown time and time again that those who practice meditation are better able to manage stress, and studies focusing on anxiety disorders have shown direct positive improvement. and starting young will ensure your brain retains more volume as you age. Those who regularly practice mindfulness will also find they have a thicker hippocampus and as a result have an easier time learning and retaining more information. They will also notice that the part of the amygdala which controls fear, anxiety, and stress is less active. Simply put, meditation has a real, measurable effect.

Beyond the physical changes, regularly practicing mindfulness has been shown to decrease instances of participant's minds getting stuck in negative thought patterns while at the same time increasing focus. This should not come as a surprise given the fact that a recent Johns Hopkins study found that regularly practicing mindfulness meditation is equally effective at treating depression, ADD and anxiety. It also improves verbal reasoning skills as shown in a study which found that GRE students who practiced mindfulness performed up to 16 points better than their peers.

However, to reap these benefits you need to meditate regularly, not just when you're feeling anxious. Think of it as a muscle: the more often you use it, the stronger it becomes. In fact, with enough time and practice, you will likely find that you are able to maintain a mild meditative state even when you are otherwise focused on the world around you. This is known as a state of mindfulness and it should be the end goal of everyone who is new to the meditative practice. Being mindful means always being connected to a calming and soothing mental state as well as one that is full of joy and peace which benefits not just yourself but everyone around you.

Practice, practice, practice: In order to practice mindfulness meditation, the first thing you are going to want to do is to pick a time that you are going to be able to practice at regularly and stick to it no matter what. When it comes to building a habit like mindfulness meditation, it is important to work on building a routine as quickly as possible. It takes 30 days for a new habit to cement itself in your life and doing it consistently will make that 30 days go by much more smoothly than it otherwise would.

Start this way: for just a few minutes, take a seat. It need not be in a chair, nor do you need to sit with your legs positioned in a specific way. Simply sit down with your back straight. Put your hands in your lap and close your eyes. Then, breathe slowly. When you do, focus all of your attention on how breathing itself feels. Really fixate on the senses: the air entering and exiting your nostrils or mouth; the expansion of your lungs, how cold or warm the air is. When these few minutes are up, open your eyes and examine how you feel physically and mentally. Try this once a day, extending the time a little bit each day.

With practice, you will be able to reliably practice mindfulness virtually anywhere, but for now, you will want all the help you can get. The end goal with mindfulness meditation is to quiet the mind as a means of finding an internal calm regardless of what might be going on in the outside world.

EMOTIONAL INTELLIGENCE AND COGNITIVE BEHAVIORAL THERAPY

It is difficult for many people to reach that state right out of the gate, however, which is why many people find a great way to get to be putting all of your effort in to taking in all of the information your senses are providing you with at once. Your senses are always providing you with a constant stream of sensory data that your brain, by and large, filters out. With mindfulness meditation, you make a conscious choice to let all of that information in, starting with deep breaths.

You are going to want to start by breathing in fully, using your diaphragm, until your lungs are completely full. As you do so, feel your lungs expand as the air enters them, consider the temperature of the air and the smells that it brings along with it. As you breathe out, feel your lungs contract and feel the way the air flows out of your body.

Make an effort to avoid judging what you feel: When you first begin practicing mindfulness meditation it is perfectly natural for your mind to intrude with thoughts about your current surroundings or to fill the void you are trying to achieve with a constant stream of consciousness. This occurs because over the years you have trained your brain to constantly be moving from one thought to the next in a rush to reach some conclusion or another.

When you find these errant thoughts breaching your sense of mental calm it is important to not interact with them as much as possible and instead to let them simply float away without interacting with them. If you find yourself getting sidetracked it is important to not attach a judgment to what has happened and to instead simply center yourself once more and continue as before. While this step is the most difficult for many people, it is important to keep it up until it becomes second nature as any interaction with the stray thoughts, even if it is just to chastise yourself for getting off track is an easy way to let even more thoughts through which will make it more difficult to find the state of mind that you are looking for.

Keep at it: When you first begin practicing mindfulness meditation it is important to do so with the right level of expectations regarding your results. Specifically, you will want to keep in mind that your mind is likely to wander frequently and that you will need to persevere through these periods if you are ever going to reach the level of mental quiet that you are looking for. To understand the ultimate mindset that you are striving for, you may find it helpful to consider the period of blankness the mind enters after a question has been asked but before the answer comes to you.

Reflect: After you have gotten into the habit of viewing the true nature of a situation without any cognitive biases standing in your way, you will then want to write down all of the specifics you noticed in as dry and factual a way as possible. Keeping your descriptions emotionless and factual will make it easier to look back at them clearly in the future, regardless of how clouded your mind is with emotion at the moment. Especially early on, taking the time to actually write out your list will make it easier for this step to become a habit as you will have the physical action to connect to rather than stray thoughts.

The goal with this practice is to become as truly invested in the things that you experience each and every day as possible. This will, in turn, make it more difficult for negative thoughts to sneak in past your defenses and start to alter the actions that you would take when compared to how you would act if you were completely free of their influence. This doesn't mean that you can't stop and smell the roses, it only means that you should take precautions to ensure that your mind remains active if you know that when it is at rest is when the trouble starts.

When keeping track of the things that are going on around you, it is important to take special care to prevent yourself from judging the things that are happening, especially when it comes to arbitrary binary concepts like unfair and fair or good and bad. Rather, you will find the process more effective if everything you write down is truly impartial as this will give you a more useful outlook on the world overall, one that

EMOTIONAL INTELLIGENCE AND COGNITIVE BEHAVIORAL THERAPY

is in no-way influenced by feelings and emotions when it is not appropriate for this to be the case.

Practice mindfulness at all times: Once you get the hang of the basics of mindfulness meditation you will find that there is practically nothing you can't do that doesn't lend itself to being mindful. The following are some of the easiest ways to get into the habit of practicing mindfulness meditation around your home, but you can also practice at work, on public transportation, or even while driving. With a little extra practice, the wide variety of times you can easily slip into a mindful state are sure to surprise you.

While it may seem surprising, if you go about doing so in the right way, spending time with Facebook or Instagram can actually be a very mindful experience. While it is easy to get distracted from your goal while interacting with social media, with practice you will find that the time you spend doing so can leave you feeling quite centered and ready to face the next challenge that awaits you.

In order for this type of mindfulness to be effective, the first thing you are going to want to do is to limit potential distractions as much as you can. This is crucial due to the fact that most people interact with social media while multitasking which will make practicing mindfulness much more difficult. Once you have cleared the distractions out of the way you will then want to clear your mind and focus on the moment as much as possible. After you have found the correct mindset, you will then want to revisit old pictures from activities you were a part of and try your hardest to relive those events as thoroughly as possible.

With each picture you see, do your best to try and remember everything you were doing at the moment. Think back to the way you felt and really let the experience wash over you. Throw yourself back into the moment with all your might and remember the various signals your mind was bombarding you with at the time.

Chapter 9: EQ at Work

In addition to the many personal benefits that emotional intelligence has to offer, it can also bring a variety of benefits to the workplace and its stakeholders at all level and across all functions. For starters, it makes it far easier for leaders to motivate their individual employees as they are far more likely to be able to accurately gauge their true motivations. It will also help to improve the collaborative process of teams of all sizes while also avoiding the potential issues that arise when groupthink takes over. Overall, it will also make it far easier for leaders to locate and act on potential opportunities they may have otherwise missed.

EQ in the workplace is also extremely useful when it comes to conflict resolution as it makes it easier for all of the involved parties to come to conclusions that are sure to work for everyone. Even better, studies show that it tends to produce higher overall levels of morale among employees that further aids them in working as effectively as possible.

EQ and hiring: While even the most technical of skills can be taught reliably, it is far more difficult to teach a new employee how to improve their EQ if they aren't already familiar with the process. Thus, companies will find it far more useful to integrate checks for EQ early on as opposed to trying to build it from scratch at a later point. For example, testing for EQ at an entry-level position and then again as a prerequisite for advancement is far easier than trying to force someone into a position and then hoping their EQ can keep up after the fact. While it will certainly require more work initially, in the end, stakeholders that have a higher overall EQ are going to be more likely to have true leadership potential making them the better choice every single time.

While there is no role in a company that won't benefit from someone with high EQ in some capacity, this doesn't mean that they all require high amounts of EQ to succeed right out of the gate. Generally speaking, the further up the corporate ladder a new-hire is, the more useful they will be if they EQ is already well-developed. Beyond this general rule, those in PR or HR are far more likely to benefit from EQ regardless of the experience required for the position. This is why vetting these individuals for their current EQ can ultimately maximize their contributions as new employees.

EQ on a global scale: In broad terms, the global economy is defined by its extreme interconnectivity through a wide variety of types of communication, collaboration, and negotiation which is why it should come as no surprise that EQ is growing in importance on the global scale as well. While there will always be a role for traditional IQ in technical positions, even these are requiring an increasing amount of contact on a larger scale which means that once again EQ is growing in importance here as well.

EQ and team building: When it comes to replicating a successful team, it is important to understand what role EQ plays in creating teams that truly work well together. This can be explained more easily by considering a competent art student. If this student was told to paint a copy of one of the great masters, the average person would not be able to tell the difference. They will never become the next van Gogh without understanding the theory behind the work and the soul that goes into it as well.

While creating a truly successful team will require more than just mimicking the required processes that have worked for other, you will find that if you focus on finding those with high EQ you can ensure you allow for a scenario where the team will develop successfully on its own. Conditions required for this sort of scenario to come to fruition include fostering group identity, encouraging trust and promoting group efficacy. When it comes to creating these conditions in a new team, consider the following:

- Having a leader is important. First things first, it is important to designate a leader that has a high level of EQ as this will help the group to reach its full potential. Doing so will also make it possible for the group to waste less time as they won't need to sort out for themselves who is going to be in charge. If you are going to be the leader in this scenario then you will have to brush up on your conflict resolution skills so that you can reliably handle arguments without risking the structure of the team as a whole.

Beyond that, you will need to ensure that you get into the habit of responding to everyone you work with in a polite, respectful fashion regardless of the scenario you find yourself in at the moment. A big part of this is also going to be listening more than you speak which is a habit that far fewer leaders cultivate than they should. A good leader is someone that not only asks for feedback but then takes it to heart when they receive it. Likewise, it is important that you avoiding making any excuses for your mistakes and instead own up to them come what may. It is also important to ensure you develop a reputation as someone who is willing to pitch in and lend a hand as needed.

- Be aware of the strengths and weaknesses your team possesses. If you are going to be an effective team leader then it is important to make sure your team feels as though they are more to you than simple cogs in the company machine which starts by ensuring you know more about them than their function and job title. While you may find it difficult to stick to this level of focus while still dealing with a very tight deadline, never forget that your employees are unique individuals who deserve to be treated as such. What's more, they all likely have lesser known or hidden talents which means the only way you can ever expect to reliably get the

most out of those who work under you is if you get to know them well enough to bring these skills to the fore.
- When it comes to ensuring you know your team as well as possible it is important that you make the extra effort to do so outside of work so you can really see what all they have to offer. This will also mean that you need to look past any first impressions you might have of individual team members and put your EQ to full use in order to determine who they really are on the inside. As a general rule, however, you will need to make it clear that you reward innovation with recognition to ensure that you see the best results possible. You will also want to make it clear that mistakes are fine as long as they aren't made due to inattention and as long as something can be learned from the accident in the first place.
- It is important that the team remains passionate about their current project in order to keep things working as smoothly as possible. To ensure this is possible it is important to either hire or gather team members who are like minded when it comes to things like corporate culture and the work they are currently doing.

No matter how in-sync and focused a team might be, however, it is only natural that they still loose focus every now and again. To help keep the team's energy up, it is important that EQ is put to use in order to determine what team members need an additional boost and call them out for their hard work accordingly. You may also find it useful to utilize your EQ in order to create an effective alternative work environment that helps to engage your team more effectively. It is also important to do what you can in order to ensure the importance of the task ahead is clear to everyone from the start which will help ensure everyone remains united in their desire for success.

- The best teams are also those that have a clear team culture. In order to manage successfully using EQ, it is important to understand that even the smallest acts can make a big difference. This is different than creating a scenario where overtime is considered mandatory or every idea that any team member has required elaborate consideration and buy in from everyone else in order to move forward. Likewise, it doesn't mean creating a workplace where everyone is completely in harmony at all times because that type of workplace, frankly, doesn't exist.

Instead, it is important to strive and creak a workplace where everyone actively seeks to work together harmoniously, while at the same time understanding that such a high bar will very rarely be maintained for very long. It is important to offer team members a healthy way to release their tensions as this will ensure that everyone is able to continue treating one another with respect. While the leader will need to create new rules now and then, it is important to only resort to this course of action when you know they connect to the core values the team has already approved of.

Guidelines created in this way are more likely to be supported by the team while also reinforcing the goals of the company as well. The end result is then that everyone is sure to feel more comfortable doing what they can to uphold these rules when appropriate.

- It is also the leader's job to help team members to successfully mange the stress that comes as part of the job as well. Too

EMOTIONAL INTELLIGENCE AND COGNITIVE BEHAVIORAL THERAPY

much stress means that even the best employee can end up feeling burned out which can ultimately lead to serious health issues if not treated properly. Thus it is very important to treat the dangers of stress seriously so that you can deal with them before they become to serious. To ensure the team's level of stress remains where it should be, there are a few easy things you can do. For starters, the team will need to have a detailed schedule that needs to be followed at each step of the process. While taking extra time to do a job properly is fine, over extending a given deadline is a slippery slope that can make it difficult for the team to finish a larger project on time and should be considered only an emergency measure. Creating the schedule ahead of time will also make it possible to give the team all the breaks they need to remain as fresh as possible so they can continue working at peak efficiency indefinitely.

It is also important to discourage multitasking as, for many jobs, it actually ends up making them take longer and generates subpar results than simply working on the two tasks back to back. Thus it is more effective to provide your team the timeframes they need to work on their projects one at a time in the long run.

- You will also need to be aware that your team is unlikely to get along harmoniously at all times, regardless of your best efforts. Luckily, you will also find that taking the time to confront these issues head on will make it possible to not only address them in a way that ensures they are wrapped up nicely, but it will also ensure they are dealt with as quickly as possible as well. When such issues are dealt with in an effective way up front it naturally reduces the stress of the team as a whole and allows them to focus on completing their

current project to the best of their abilities.
- Finally, it is important that you put your EQ to good use in order to understand the true motivations of your team so you can actively do your part in order to ensure everyone is dedicated to the idea of working as hard as possible. You can also use your EQ to help them overcome any unexpected challenges that they might currently be facing. Remember, as the leader, it is your job to keep each and every member of your team feeling as though their voice is heard. This means you will need to use your EQ in order to help them develop improved communication skills by letting them work on their active listening skills and improving their mastery of body language or simply giving them an opportunity to vent when needed. What this doesn't mean is that you should give them free reign to give into their negative emotions, however, as this is the sort of thing that can easily drag an entire team down if left unchecked. Instead, it is important to channel any of this type of negativity into an opportunity to discuss the problem in question, with the entire team, in order to come up with the best possible solution.

Chapter 10: Improve Your Leadership Skills

If you are a manager or one of the leaders in a company, you will find that emotional intelligence can serve you well. You can use this skill to assess what your employee needs without them suffering or getting mad because they feel ignored. You are able to use this intelligence in order to understand the impact of decisions on your staff and you can manage expectations, both your own and theirs, more effectively, take action so that friction is kept to a minimum, and even answer questions when they arise. Managers who are emotionally intelligent are the ones who will listen to their employees without feeling attacked or taking things too personally.

At times, you will have to deal with a conflict in the workplace. Those who have emotional intelligence have worked on increasing their self-control and this can be so helpful when it comes to avoiding conflicts in the workplace. You will be able to approach the conflict and assess your own feelings before reacting so you come up with a result that makes everyone happy.

When looking at your workplace level of emotional intelligence, start by considering these three important patterns:

The team handles small issues internally without involving the boss

Small issues are those that tend to be personal in nature and do not involve the task at hand in a significant way. Ideally, these issues should be handled between the individuals where they arise and they will never escalate all the way up to management proper. If your HR department or a team leader is regularly required to ensure that team members stop bickering and get back to work, your workplace emotional intelligence is definitely suffering.

Understanding the line between small issues and large issues can be tricky, which is why it helps to look for patterns. If team members are constantly finding new things to argue about, even if they don't reach management, then there is a deeper issue at play somewhere in the organization. If you are having difficulty determining the root of the problem, ask around, patterns should emerge regarding core issues if you look hard enough.

Team members are empowered to make decisions

A good sign of emotional intelligence in the workplace is team members with the agency to choose the right course of action for a given situation and implement it without going to several layers of approval beforehand. Team members in this scenario will feel they are trusted and will work harder as a result and leaders will have more time to ensure everything is running smoothly without having to micromanage decisions that are being made constantly.

This is an easy pattern to identify, all you need to do is chart a few decisions that have been made in the workplace recently and look at the chain of approval on each. It shouldn't take long to determine a pattern and work to implement changes as needed.

Determine your personal leadership style

Coercive leader: This type of leader tends to take an aggressive stance which means they also need to have a very high EQ if they want their team to work well together as opposed to planning a mutiny. They most frequently dictate directives and order team members around, expecting everyone to fall in line automatically. While not effective in most common situations, this style is extremely effective for teams working with dangerous or time sensitive projects where a more inclusive leadership style simply wouldn't be feasible. In order for this type of leadership style to work in the long-term, the leader needs to see better than average results at every turn. Teams that develop around this type of leader are often very tightknit and spend time together improving their cohesiveness both on the job and off.

Authoritative leader: This type of leader typically got to where they are today because they have a specific vision or goal in mind that other people naturally fall in line behind. This type of leadership style tends to really shine when the team is currently at a crossroads as to the best way to move forward effectively. Authoritative leaders tend to use their EQ when it comes to crafting their vision statement so they can get as many people as possible on board for the greater good. It will also be useful when it comes to getting everyone to see the big picture to ensure that things continue to run smoothly even when they are not their to directly oversee the details.

Affiliative leader: This leader type typically excels at creating a team that works with little to no external input. They tend to make a habit of always putting the team first, regardless of what else might be taking place and they are quick to dole out praise and positive feedback in equal measure. If the team existed prior to the new leader being brought on, and they were barely holding things together, then this is an effective leadership style to get things back on track while also almost guaranteeing a performance boost at the same time. This style tends to falter in the long-term, however, as it tends to let minor negative performance issues go untreated as long as the big issues are being dealt with which can ultimately lead to new issues forming in the long run.

Democratic leader: This type of leader is one that tends to place all the major decisions the team has to face to the team as a whole. Thus, it is vital that this team leader's EQ is on point in order to ensure they can convince the team that their desired course of action is the one that is ultimately followed. This type of leadership style requires a very strong leader who is able to stand up to the pressure that this type of environment creates. When done correctly, however, it can dramatically boost morale as team members feel as though they are really contributing to the culture of the team as a whole. It can quickly lead to unproductivity if the leader is not firmly in control, however, so it is best used with caution.

Three steps to improve your communication skills as a leader

Watch your body language: Humans are social creatures by nature which means all anyone is ever really trying to do is to ensure that other people like them. Keeping this in mind, it then becomes much easier to influence others by using body language to appeal to their need for acceptance.

Nodding is an odd reaction in that it is subconsciously linked to feelings of agreement, both when the feelings occur first before the action takes place, and also when they occur second. What's more, when you nod at someone, they will then be presented with the subconscious urge to nod back. Taken together, this means that if you ask someone to do something while already nodding, the other person is more likely to start nodding back immediately and then subconsciously relate this action to a feeling of agreement.

Standing while speaking physically provides you with more perspective on the situation which anyone currently sitting will subconsciously relate to a greater degree of power. Power equates to influence which means you are more likely to be persuasive over others while standing above them. Above does not mean directly overhead, however, as violating someone's personal space is a good way to get that person to discount the point you are trying to make.

Touch is the most communal of all the senses and creating a physical bond with another person is a great way to ensure that they are more likely to initially treat you as an equal. Studies show that as little as 3 seconds of skin to skin contact is likely to make the other party more responsive to a given interaction which means you should get in the habit of shaking hands with every single person you meet, just in case.

In most situations, you will find that the other party is going to be more agreeable to whatever it is you are saying if you lower your voice instead of raising it. Additionally, you will want to perform the following exercise before you have any intense, face to face interaction time planned. Simply take 30 seconds and repeat the phrase "um hum" aloud without opening your mouth.

This exercise will stretch your vocal cords and ensure you sound your best once you do speak. Follow this exercise up by speaking in a clear, but slightly quite, voice to ensure that the other party is actively listening to everything you have to say. This level of attention ensures that you control the conversation in question and makes it more likely the other party will agree with you once you are finished speaking.

Finally, be sure to open up as a defensive, closed body posture automatically tells those around you that you are tense, nervous and unwilling to come to a mutually beneficial agreement. This isn't a secret science either, these are common body language cues that everyone will pick up on to some degree, even if this is just subconsciously.

What's worse, once they are aware of them, most team members will start mimicking them, and their related behaviors as well. Closed body posture gives them the signal that there's something to worry about and they'll fell ill at ease and much more resistant to persuasion. The fix, luckily, is quite simple. If you concerned you may be displaying a defensive body posture, all you need to do is sit up straight so that your spine is aligned, and your shoulders are squared. At the same time, you are going to want to breathe deeply, place your hands on your legs, with your palms up. While this isn't a natural position, it is an important part of the overall whole.

Opening up your posture in this way will also serve to improve your mental state by decreasing the amount of the hormone cortisol that your body produces. Cortisol is responsible for stress levels so in this case acting and outwardly appearing to be calm and collected will make you feel this way as well, relaxing your team members in the process.

Keep your exchanges focused: Remember the seven Cs. Be clear as to what your goal is for the conversation. Be concise, everyone on your team no doubt has a to-do list a mile long, keep things short and your team will love you for it. Be concrete, your team will only benefit from clear goals based on data, ensure you stay on message and stick to the facts. Be correct, taking the time to double check your facts will lead to your team to trust you not to make mistakes in the long run.

Be coherent, before you discuss important topics with your team take the time to go over it first in your head to ensure everything makes sense, your team will appreciate it. Complete, before discussing project specifics or new policies ensure you have all the information you need, sticking to this goal will increase productivity. Be courteous, this should go without saying but take the time to be courteous and polite to your team, it will only lead to positive results.

Listen, no really listen: Many people get in the habit, especially at work, of taking the time their coworkers are speaking to merely think over what it is they are going to say next. As a leader, you do not have that luxury. You must hear your team when they come to you with concerns about the current project or thoughts on how to make it better.

What's more, as you gain a reputation for really hearing your team they will come to you with more and more information, giving you the chance to practice listening all the more, thus ensuring the cycle repeats. No on leads from a vacuum and no single person can account for all the possibilities in a single project. Take the time to hear what your team has to contribute and ensure that you have all the angles covered.

If the goal of the current action is to come to a mutual decision, then a good first step is to go out of your way to make it clear you are listening to what the other person is saying. The other party is much more likely to actively participate in finding a joint solution if they feel as though their contributions are being heard and taken to heart. Maintain eye contact while they are speaking while leaning in to indicate you want to hear every word and you will have them giving off nonverbal cues indicating how comfortable they are in no time flat.

Chapter 11: Mistakes to Avoid

Using too many labels: Before you become too familiar with your emotional tendencies, it can be extremely tempting to hide behind the types of labels that make it easy to avoid doing any real work on your foibles. Things like grumpy, headstrong, impatient, etc. are little more than the mental equivalent of telling a child they are big-boned. While it might save them some heartache in the short-term, in the long-term it is doing far more harm than good.

This is why it is so important to banish these labels during the self-assessment phase as if you don't you can accidentally leave negative habits in place simply because you feel like they are a personality trait as opposed to a negative mindset that needs purging. If you aren't sure if a specific quirk is a character trait or a negative mindset simply apply it to another person and then ask yourself what you would think of the person who had it.

Not choosing your friends wisely: When it comes to improving your mindset once and for all, you will be surprised at how much those you associate with most regularly directly affect your mindset for the positive or for the negative. Practically, what this means is that if you find your EQ not progressing as quickly as you might like then you may do well to take a look around and see if you can't find the reason why staring back at you.

Focusing on what you can't change: If you find yourself wasting valuable time replaying back things that went wrong in your past because of the way you let the emotions get the best of you, then all you are really doing is letting those same emotions continue to flutter around unchecked. Replaying such things over and over will only provide your mind with plenty of additional excuses to try and do something better the next time a similar situation arises. Rather than letting this pattern continue unabated this is a great opportunity to practice controlling your emotions as effectively as possible as opposed to letting them control you once again.

If you find dealing with this type of pattern to be particularly difficult, instead of focusing on the situation the way you remember it, try looking at things with a more clinical eye. Doing so will often reveal weaknesses that were previously overlooked, or potentially a path to success that can be utilized the next time you end up doing something similar. It is crucial that you remain vigilant for these for these situations as well as the longstanding beliefs that they may come into conflict with to ensure things are revised as needed. Only by closely monitoring yourself to keep up your positive outlook will you be able to make the most of all of the hard work you have done to get to this point.

Getting too focused on winning a conversation: While everyone likes to be right, the fact is, 95 percent of all conversations aren't going to have clear winners and losers. Not only that but thinking about things in this type of binary fashion will only make it more difficult for you to build your EQ to the point that you can easily experience empathy for others. If you spend too much time thinking in terms of winners and losers you run the risk of taking mild disagreements too far in hopes of coming out on top over something that ultimately doesn't matter much one way or the other.

Regardless of how it might feel in the moment, this is really just a clear sign that your emotions are running rampant because if you were correctly managing the relationship in question then you would be working towards an outcome that works for both parties, regardless of who did what to reach the current stalemate. Remember to choose your battles and to avoid drawing lines in the sand that don't need to be there.

Confusing aggressive behavior and assertive behavior: One of the secrets of being emotionally intelligent is learning to be more assertive without being aggressive. Assertive people know how not to please people all the time without offending them. Assertiveness is a reasonable and genuine statement of opinions and feelings. "I would really prefer going to the games this weekend." This is an assertive statement.

You are making your needs clear without being aggressive or demanding. Aggressiveness is marked by a clear lack of respect for the needs and rights of other people. When you are aggressive, you are looking at things only from a selfish perspective or seeking to satisfy a self-filling goal. The aggressive version of the above statement would be, "we're good for the games this weekend."

You are pronouncing your statement more like a judgment without respect or concern for the other person.

On the other hand, assertiveness is characterized by respect and understanding for the other person's feelings or opinion, even though you may not agree with it. While aggressive says, "Only I am right", assertive says, "Though your opinion doesn't agree with mine, I respect it. We can agree to disagree."

Assertive people don't let others take advantage of them and know where to draw the line without being harsh. They know when to say "no" to people without hurting people's feelings. When you demonstrate respect for a person or group of people, the hurt is reduced. Assertive is making your stand clear while showing respect.

However, when you display a lack of respect or concern for the other person's feelings, opinion or desires, you are treading on aggression. Assertive people are unafraid of standing up for their values. They don't shy away from expressing their needs and goals to others. Assertive folks treat others as equals and operate from the point of mutual respect. They don't intend to hurt people and themselves. These are the people who are always seeking a win-win situation.

Especially when you are actively working to build up your emotional intelligence for the first time, making a habit of not speaking up for yourself reinforces negative habits including fearing what others will think when you do speak up for yourself, and modifying your behavior to suit the needs of others. Regardless of how it manifests itself, or how major or minor the slight might be, it is important to never take it lying down and always let others know that you are an important human being who deserves to be heard.

Before you move forward and assert your importance in the given situation it is important to take another moment and run down the reasons why it is you feel you have been wronged and are in need of restitution. You only have a brief window to connect with the other party in most scenarios, don't waste them fumbling for the right words to convey the legitimate injustice that has been perpetrated against you. Don't jump straight to attack mode, explain the situation rationally and expect the other person to do the same. If they fail to respond in kind, express your self-confidence and escalate the importance of your request appropriately.

Once you have decided that you are certainly in the right, gather your thoughts as well as your energy. It is important to assert yourself in this situation using authoritative body language. Stand up straight, hold your head up high, relax your arms and plant your feet. When working to get the other person's attention, speak in a clear and commanding voice that is loud enough for the other person to surely hear but not exceedingly loud for the location you find yourself in. It is important to always address the other person politely and to give them every chance at reasonable discourse.

It is important to always express your feelings directly in a way that clearly elucidates the problem you have and what you expect the other person to do to resolve the situation. To be self-confident you don't need to always walk away the victor, expressing yourself appropriately is a victory in and of itself. This is why it is important to always collect yourself before you address the situation head on, you only have one chance to make a first impression, you want it to be a good one. Have a clear idea of your plan of attack as it will otherwise be easy for the other person to simply dismiss your complaint offhand.

EMOTIONAL INTELLIGENCE AND COGNITIVE BEHAVIORAL THERAPY

Not having SMART goals

Emotionally intelligent people know what they want to achieve in life because they live and breathe this in and out. This does not only mean goals in career but in life, whether it is a happy marriage, a fulfilling career in a non-profit, feeding the hungry, becoming a humanitarian and son on. Start prepping yourself by writing your goals down- this has to everything that you want to accomplish in your life. Run a full marathon? Write it down! Scale the base camp of Mt. Everest? Write it down. Buy a house? Write it down. This will eventually turn into a long list so look at what you've written down and pick a dream or two that you feel most passionate about and apply the SMART goal setting approach which is:

S: SMART goals are specific. The best goals are the ones that you will always be able to clearly determine where you stand in relation to the goal. The goal should then have a clearly defined fail state as well as state that will clearly let you know when you have crossed the finish line. Specific goals are also going to be much easier to chart out over time as their specificity will lend to clear sub-goals that can be linked to their success or failure.

When you choose a specific goal, you are going to want to guarantee that you have a clear idea of the following details to ensure that you have chosen a goal that is truly specific enough for your needs.

- Who you will need to work with in order to make the goal a reality
- What you will need to do in order to get started on completing the goal
- Where you will need to go in order to see the goal through to completion
- Why you wanted to get started completing the goal in the first place
- When you can realistically expect the goal to be completed

- How you will go about completing the goal in various steps

M: SMART goals are measurable. A goal which is measurable makes it easy to determine precise metrics for success, progress or failure. Keeping goals measurable will help you work through them at a steady pace rather than in fits and starts. If you are having a hard time making your goals measurable, try considering how many or how much of something might indicate success or failure. Likewise, starting from the endpoint and working backwards may be easier, consider how you will know the goal has been successfully completed and then working towards the beginning can make measure goals easier.

A: SMART goals are attainable. A good goal is not only specific and measurable; it is realistically attainable as well. All the planning and measuring in the world will never do you any good if you have decided to work towards a goal that is never going to be able to be achieved, no matter what. While setting a goal to be a be extremely emotionally intelligent is a noble goal, if you are not already halfway there then it is too pie in the sky to realistically attempt to approach at the moment. If the goal you are working for doesn't seem realistically attainable you will find it much harder to focus on it with the real determination you are going to need to see any goal through to completion, making it even more unlikely you are going to be able to attain it still. Stick with goals that remain in the realm of possibility for the best results.

R: SMART goals are relevant: When it comes to setting goals to improve your outlook on life, it is important that you start with goals that will have the most noticeable effect on your day to day life at first, and then work towards more abstract goals from there. This type of approach will have numerous benefits in both the short and the long term, ultimately culminating in a mental state that is clear of distractions and more accurately able to focus on the long term results you need to see true financial freedom.

When you are first starting out, choosing goals that will have the most immediate impact on your current situation will not only make it easier to focus on other tasks down the line once the current distractions are out of the way, it will also teach your brain to associate hard work and dedication with successfully completing goals. This, in turn, will make it easier for you to commit to more difficult or complicated goals in the long term as you will have a historical reason to equate hard work and dedication with success.

Putting it all to good use: You can create your vision board with the images and words that reflect your goals and place it where you can see every day. Include words and images that communicate how you feel about your most passionate goal. Break larger goals into actionable steps and create a plan to get started.

Along the way, also recognize the people who play a big part in your life who can help you realize these goals and milestones. Acknowledge their support as this is a step towards emotional intelligence and also do not forget to thank them for the things that they do to help you get there.

T: A SMART goal is timely: While you won't be able to tell a proper SMART goal apart from the rest by just looking at a few of its properties, you will always be able to identify one by its strict timetable including a firm start and finish date. Ultimately it will not matter how measurable, specific, relevant and attainable your goal is as without a firm timeframe for you to complete it in, the odds of it actually seeing completion drop below 20 percent.

Conclusion

Thanks for making it through to the end of *Emotional Intelligence: One Book Packed with Easy Ways to Improve Your Self-Awareness, Take Control of Your Emotions, Enhance Your Relationships and Guarantee EQ Mastery*, let's hope it was informative and able to provide you with all of the tools you need to achieve your goals, whatever it is that they may be. Just because you've finished this book doesn't mean there is nothing left to learn on the topic, and expanding your horizons is the only way to find the mastery you seek.

Now that you have finished this book, it is time to stop reading already and to get ready to get started improving your EQ once and for all. While reading through this book you no doubt came across some exercise whose value you could clearly see in your own life as well as those you felt would only bolster aspects of EQ that you already have under control. Nevertheless, it is important to keep in mind that all of the exercises discussed were included for a reason and the sum total of the exercises in order is sure to be more than its individual parts. Thus, it is important to trust the process and trust that doing so will leave your EQ as primed for success as possible.

Book 2:

Cognitive Behavioral Therapy

The Complete Guide to Using CBT to Battle Anxiety, Depression and Regaining Control over Anger, Panic, and Worry.
By: Daniel Patterson

Table of Contents

Introduction

> What exactly is CBT?
>
> How does CBT work?
>
> What Types of Problems can CBT Solve?
>
> Why is CBT Popular and Trusted?
>
> What Occurs at a CBT Session?
>
> What's CBT Training Like?
>
> How Long Does a CBT Remedy Usually Last?
>
> Are there any CBT Methods Which People can use aside from Actual Therapy Sessions?
>
> *Chapter 1: The History of Cognitive Behavioral Therapy (CBT)*
>
> Spiraling Towards Success
> The Foundational Framework of CBT
> Behavioral Therapy Roots
> Cognitive Therapy Roots
> Automatic Thoughts in Cognitive Therapy
> Combining the Approaches
>
> *Chapter 2: Is CBT the Right Therapy for You?*
> *Quick Checklist*
> *Chapter 3: The Daily Lifestyle Guide to CBT*
>
> Pleasant Activity Scheduling

Situation Exposure Hierarchies
Imagery Based Exposure
CBT Method
Cognitive Tools
Behavioral Tools
360-degree opinions
Values Clarification Exercise

Chapter 4: CBT Advantages and Methods

How Cognitive Behavior Therapy Works
Features that make CBT an Effective Tool
Pragmatic method
Cognitive Behavioral Therapy vs. Other Types of Psychotherapy
How is CBT different From Other Popular Forms of Therapy?
CBT Journal work

Chapter 5: Disorders, Medical, and Emotional Issues CBT is Expected to Treat

Panic Disorders
Depression
Attention Deficit/Hyperactivity Disorder (ADHD)
Obsessive Compulsive Disorder (OCD)
Social Phobia/Social Anxiety
Bipolar Disorder
Generalized Anxiety Disorder (GAD)
Schizophrenia
Bulimia Nervosa
Fear of Flying/Flying phobia

Chapter 6: CBT for Depression

Types of Depression

Signs and Symptoms of Depression

How Does Cognitive Behavioral Therapy (CBT) Differ From Other Depression Treatments?

How Cognitive Behavioral Therapy Can Help With Depression

Cognitive Behavioral Therapy Techniques to Counteract the Negative Thinking of Depression

Chapter 7: CBT for Anxiety

Thoughts challenging in CBT for anxiety
Exposure Therapy for Anxiety
Systematic Desensitization
Complementary Therapies for Anxiety Disorder
Making Anxiety Therapy Work for You

Chapter 8: CBT for Fear and Phobias

Treatment for Phobias
Cognitive Behavioral Therapies for Phobia's
Group Therapies to Ease Fears
Individual Therapy
Family Therapy

Chapter 9: CBT for Maladaptive or Bad Habits

Avoidance
Substance Misuse
Withdrawing
Converting Anxiety to Anger

Chapter 10: CBT for Obsession and OCD

Three aspects of CBT therapy for OCD
OCD Steps
Preparing the Way for Your Patient
What Your Patients Can Expect?

Chapter 11: CBT for Intrusive Thoughts and OCD

Relationship Intrusive Thoughts
Sexual Sensitive Thoughts
Magical Thinking about Intrusive Thoughts
Religious Intrusive Thoughts
Violent Intrusive Thoughts
Body-focused Obsession (sensorimotor OCD)
Symmetry and Orderliness
Acronyms commonly used for OCD
Treatment of OCD Intrusive Thoughts Using CBT

Chapter 12: CBT for Mental Health and Exercise

Cognitive Tools & Exercise
Behavioral Tools & Exercise
Tools from Third-Wave Therapies
Mental Health Ailments that may improve with CBT
Handle grief
The Downward Spiral of Mental Disorder

Chapter 13: CBT for Self-Monitoring & Progress Evaluation

The CBT Toolbox
Using CBT to Achieve Success
Defining Success
SMART Goals & Action Plan

Chapter 14: How CBT Deals With Things

Getting the Most out of it

Chapter 15: Final Thoughts on Cognitive Behavioral Therapy

What Next For the Future of CBT?
How Many CBT Sessions Will You Need to Get the Desired Result?
Is CBT limited in Any Way?
Learning About Your Emotional Health Condition
What You May Anticipate

Identify Strategies to Manage Emotions

Ways to Practice Cognitive Behavioral Therapy Techniques on Your Own
Make Sure That You know:

Conclusion

Introduction

You might have heard of cognitive behavioral therapy (CBT)—the evidence-based psychotherapy procedure dedicated to changing unwanted ideas and behaviors—before. It seems to be cited in virtually every informative article on the web: Insomnia issues? Try CBT. Struggling with trauma? CBT will provide help. For stress, depression, very low self-esteem, anxiety about traveling, etc., CBT may be your answer. There's a high probability that you have received CBT or that you may even know somebody that has.

So what is CBT? Does it genuinely alleviate emotional distress and how does it achieve this? Yes, it does and the exact methods may be puzzling for some.

What exactly is CBT?

CBT is just one of the dozens of remedy options utilized in psychotherapy. It truly is centered upon the premise that a lot of life's issues come from defective notions (that is precisely where "cognitive" stems from) and behaviors. By deliberately altering them to healthier, more successful objectives, we could ease distress. In training, CBT is commonly composed of pinpointing both the controversial views and behaviors, and replacing them with responses that are wholesome.

CBT is a type of communicating therapy that helps to identify difficult thoughts, and also supports many people to mostly know how to pattern their thinking and even their behaviors, ultimately improving their way of feeling. This investigates the relationship that occurs between behaviors, feelings, and thoughts. Therefore, it arises from two very different schools of psychology: Cognitive therapy, and behaviorism. The roots of these can be trailed to two models.

CBT is also defined as the joining together of both behavioral and cognitive therapies, with empirical support strong enough to be deemed as medical care for many physiological disorders.

CBT also focuses on building a person's personal skills, or matching skills that will empower them to become conscious of feelings and thoughts, and identifying solutions. It also has a way of impacting people's perception, aiding the improvement of bad feelings by replacing behaviors and beliefs. CBT is different from other traditional methods of talk therapy as it gives a determined prominence to the individual's acquired skills and the use of assignments. This therapy aims not just to solve any individual's current problem or to work on the negativity of their thoughts but to assist in improving the toolkit of the individual to become efficient in solving problems that may arise in the near future.

How does CBT work?

CBT, unlike psychoanalytic and psychodynamic therapies, is a short-term approach that usually takes as little as 6 sessions, or even up to 20 sessions. All through every session, you and your therapist might identify situations and circumstances within your life that might have caused your low mood, or contributed to it. This is when your current way of thinking and your distorted perception can be tackled and identified. You might be encouraged to save journals to keep records of each of your life events and your reactions to them. This might also assist the therapist to break down and identify your thoughts and reactions, which may include:

- All for nothing thinking which views the world as black or white.

- Rejecting the positives, which might disqualify every positive experience and feeling that you've had.

- Overgeneralization, which means drawing broad conclusions regarding a particular event.

- Automatic negative thoughts i.e. when you experience scolding thoughts.

- Taking things just too personally i.e. thinking that some things happen due to what you say, what you've done, or a feeling that everyone's actions are mostly directed to you.

- Unrealistically reducing or increasing the usefulness of every event, which means building up or bringing things down in a way that might not match the real world.

- Focusing on a negative issues i.e. dwelling on things to the point whereby your general perception is very dark.

What Types of Problems can CBT Solve?

CBT can be employed for stress, depression, injury, self-esteem problems, ADHD, inferior communication, or unrealistic expectations of one's partner, to name a few. When it's a problem that entails notions and behaviors, CBT acts as a cure.

Why is CBT Popular and Trusted?

A reason for CBT being so popular and trusted is that it's been analyzed so broadly. It's worth researching about as it highlights fast and solution-oriented interventions; its intention is always to generate distinct and quantifiable adjustments in notions and behaviors, and it is seen as a goldmine for therapists.

What Occurs at a CBT Session?

At the start, the therapist is likely to mention a method of payment, the cancellation policies, the aims for the therapy, the client therapy report, plus a summary of the client's problems. From then on, the discussions will be around the battles that the client faces and how to alleviate them.

The therapist and client interact to generate an action program for whatever problem the client is facing. An activity plan signifies that they establish the debatable notions and behaviors, discover an easy method to improve them and produce a way to execute this plan.

What's CBT Training Like?

CBT relies on offering an instant and efficient decrease of outward symptoms. Regular training may incorporate exercises a keeping a diary of ideas and feelings. It may also incorporate methods aimed a particular subject, examining relevant publications or searching out circumstances to employ your new strategy.

How Long Does a CBT Remedy Usually Last?

One of the highlights of CBT is that it is centered on eradicating signs and indicators as speedily as possible, on average in a month or two—depending on the patient's ability to focus in therapy, and the quantity and seriousness of their problems. Brevity is crucial for the particular approach; an essential feature that stands CBT out from other therapies.

Are there any CBT Methods Which People can use aside from Actual Therapy Sessions?

Perhaps you have kept a gratitude diary? Have you thought about tracking your junk food intake? Have you ever monitored your sleep patterns and its quality?

If you've done any of these, you are already employing a few of the fundamentals of CBT into your daily activity. However, personalized and structured therapy remains the best.

A lot of information will be shared in this book to help anyone showing symptoms that CBT could alleviate. The importance of CBT cannot be overemphasized, and so let's delve deeper!

Chapter 1: The History of Cognitive Behavioral Therapy (CBT)

CBT has become well-known over the years as many people are now very much aware of its use and efficacy in treating known disorders like depression and anxiety. This is not a new therapy whatsoever, and it has a structure that makes it easy to measure the results—factors that have made it easy to have many successful clinical trials and as a treatment that is endorsed and used for the UK's NHS.

Spiraling Towards Success

In the 1960s, a psychiatrist by the name of Aaron T. Beck treated individuals who were suffering from depression. He wanted to understand better the legitimacy of psychoanalysis methods made famous by Sigmund Freud. Though Beck started doing some research and experiments with the hope of verifying the relevant treatments techniques, he discovered that the methods had very little or no positive effects on patients that were depressed. Upon finding this great stunning revelation, Beck had no other choice than to develop other new and effective methods to assist his patients. As a result, with the aid of other known, celebrated figures like Albert Ellis, Beck developed the treatment methods of CBT.

Since Dr. Beck first started treating his depressed patients with his newly developed therapeutic methods, CBT became one of the highest regarded treatments for mental health.

With the modernized structure of CBT today, there are other various therapeutic activities that psychiatrists can use not just to help their patients prevail over depression but also other health disorders, such as obesity, addiction, and anxiety.

While it might be easy to think that CBT can only be used by medical professionals in treating those with mental health struggles, this isn't the case. The structure of CBT is built on fundamental psychological beliefs that can be applied to anyone.

The Foundational Framework of CBT

Before looking in depth at the other ways that we can use CBT's tools and exercise for our personal development, it's important to gain a better understanding of the treatment's methods and their underlying structure.

For those that do not have prior knowledge of CBT, the most important thing is that CBT therapists work with patients at the cognition and behavioral levels—the "C" and "B" parts of CBT. Beyond this fundamental point, it's imperative to briefly examine the four concepts that stand as the background of which CBT is built upon—The CBT triangle, automatic thoughts, dysfunctional thinking, and the cognitive model.

The CBT triangular model explains how an individual's emotions, thoughts, and behaviors affect everyone. A CBT therapist always sees the triangle as one of the psychological facts that guides all of humanity.

The CBT therapist starts working with patients to form the treatment methods with the understanding that all individuals' behaviors, thoughts, and emotions affect one another continuously, at all times. For example, when an individual begins to think badly, there will be severe repercussions at the behavioral and emotional level. Likewise, if an individual behaves destructively, there will be severe ramifications at the emotional and cognitive level.

Since cognitive thoughts do not affect our behaviors and emotions, our emotions also affect behaviors and emotions; everyone can take actions that are life-affirming at both the behavioral and cognitive levels in ways that increase the feeling of subjective well-being.

The cognitive concept of the CBT model explains how specific circumstances and situations lead to a chain reaction of body sensations, thoughts, behaviors, and emotional responses. When an individual suffers from social anxiety, they are usually in a high-pressured environment; they will be anxious about cognitions that guide their behavior. The thoughts and emotions of social anxiety have a way of influencing one another; individuals will take steps to take themselves out of the situations. The model explains to us that these situations cause thoughts that allows emotions to alter our behavior.

Lastly, the CBT concept of automatic thoughts and dysfunctional thinking are areas where a mental ailment develops. While psychiatrists and psychologists of various schools of thought will not agree on everything, they all agree that there is a flow of seemingly automatic thoughts flowing from our brains. When working with people that have a mental illness, a CBT therapist will point the finger towards every negative cognition or dysfunctional patterns of thinking as the culprits causing a behavioral and emotional disturbance.

Behavioral Therapy Roots

Treatments for behavioral disorders have been available for a long time. In the early 1900s, Pavlov, Skinner, and Watson were all early supporters of behavioral treatments. Behaviorism is rooted in the idea that every behavior can be trained, measured, and also changed. It also connotes the fact that our environment has a way of shaping our behavior.

Behavioral therapy came about at first in the 1940s, as a response to WWII veterans needing support in adjusting back into "normal" life and dealing with their horrific experience of war. It was used as a short-term therapy of anxiety and depression that corresponded with the research into how people learn to react emotionally and behave in different life situations. This confronts psychoanalytic therapy which was famous during the time and is considered as CBT's first wave.

The old behavioral therapy approach is no longer as commonly used as it was many years ago. Right now, we have a more collaborative approach to the treatment of cognitive issues, and it has proved to be more reliable.

Cognitive Therapy Roots

In the 1900s, an Australian psychotherapist's (Alfred Adler) concept of fundamental mistakes and the role they play in unpleasant emotions made him among the earliest therapists to deal with psychotherapy cognition. The work he carried out inspired the American psychologist Albert Ellis to change Rational Emotive Behavioral Therapy (REBT) in the 1950s. This is now known to be the earliest form of cognitive psychotherapy, and its fundamental idea is that a person's emotional discomfort comes from either their thoughts about an event or the event that happened itself.

In 1950-1960, the aforementioned psychiatrist Aaron T. Beck learned that most of his clients had internal communications (voices in their heads) during their therapy sessions. He also found that some clients also seemed to talk to themselves but didn't share with him what these voices said. For example, a client saying, "The therapist is quiet today. I wonder if he is not happy with me." And by that, they are already anxious about the result.

Automatic Thoughts in Cognitive Therapy

Beck knew that the usefulness of the link between feelings and thoughts. He then coined the phrase "automatic thoughts" to tell us what exactly was going on in our minds. He also found out that though many people are not conscious of these thoughts, they can learn to report and identify them; he discovered that people who are angry always have bad thoughts, and by uncovering and challenging these thoughts, there can be long-lasting positive changes. In other words, CBT assists people to come out of this automatic thought process.

In the 1960s, a series of studies empirically showed how cognition influences emotions and behaviors; this is also known as cognitive revolution and is also referred as CBT's second wave. It strictly stresses the importance that conscious thoughts play in psychotherapy.

Combining the Approaches

Behavioral therapies are also relevant in treating disorders like neurosis, but have not yet been able to overcome depression. As cognitive therapies have become more popular and psychologists are seeing more and success with them, the joining together of different approaches can be used to successfully treat panic disorders. CBT remains as placing greater emphasis on the individual's experience, belief, and feelings at every given moment.

Chapter 2: Is CBT the Right Therapy for You?

Are you puzzled about the various types of therapy that are available? If so, you are not alone. CBT is one of the best known forms of therapy, but how can it help you and what does CBT entail exactly?

Whenever I meet a client for the very first time, I ask questions about what they know about CBT and, most times, the response I get is quite the same: "Very little." This is not exactly a problem, though, as part of my job is to tell them how it works and also to take them through the process. Nevertheless, I'm sure there are more people than one realizes whom are in dire need of help and don't realize how CBT can be exactly what they need.

CBT is still relatively new and is respected everywhere because its fundamentals are based on a simple proposition that our thinking affects our feelings. This begins by developing a better understanding of how we usually think of ourselves and those around us, which might lead to an emotional disturbance.

Here, we will discuss ways in which different CBT strategies can help you to start thinking and behaving in a healthy and emotional way.

So, how will you know if CBT is appropriate for you?

I'll assume that you are reading this chapter because you are not feeling too well, and that you are struggling with your life and no longer feel your "normal" self. This might be a feeling that you have been noticing for a very long time or it might've been triggered recently. You might be aware that you are suffering from some depression or anxiety or you might also have anger issues. You might also be in a very tough personal situation, self-confidence is low or you feel alone.

Emotional problems can be in various forms, and one of the vital keys is to know if CBT can help. It can be very difficult to pull yourself together or snap out of how you feel—no matter how much you bottle it up, talk about it, or try as much as possible to ignore it, those negative thoughts and feeling always appear and seem to get worse each day. The positive, if this is how you feel, is that no matter how bad you feel, you can also change—CBT helps by establishing an equilibrium, and making necessary adjustments to make sure that things go back to normal for you, and that you develop a more helpful and positive perspective.

So, if you are looking for a therapy that follows a strategic and logical process, one that assists in changing and also moving forward the things that are holding you back, then CBT is a good option to explore. Unlike other psychoanalytic therapies that help to focus on things of the past, CBT discourses what happens presently—it takes what has happened in past events to help know or take into account why you are going through current emotional trauma, basically focusing on solutions and methods to bring about a long-term change. The philosophy that is learned can be applied through so many life circumstances.

Hence, CBT is very useful in the modern day, encouraging you to always be responsible for the way you feel, empower you with the emotional consciousness, providing effective ways to cope with difficult life challenges. We are not born with our feelings and thoughts, but they often develop as we begin to grow older, which can be influenced by our teachers, friends, our daily experiences, and parents. This will assist us to understand that we have the power to change our thoughts. And if our thoughts enhance the way we feel, we need to understand the sort of thoughts that leads us to unhelpful emotions, so that we can make the necessary changes.

A very important question to consider is how often you are used to "black and white" thinking in your life? "I must succeed. If I don't, I'm a failure," "that person did not smile back at me, so I know they don't like me." This unyielding, all-or-nothing tendency creates more pressure and is an example of a thought distortion that is more likely to be targeted for change, and to create alternatives that are more balanced.

Quick Checklist

CBT can help if:

- you want to learn and take control of your emotions
- you love the idea of a logical, scientifically-proven therapy that will help you change how you feel presently and also in the future
- you believe that change is possible even if it seems impossible at the moment
- you are happy to practice strategies between sessions
- you feel blocked and stuck

Chapter 3: The Daily Lifestyle Guide to CBT

There is a theory that if you do something consistently for 21 days it becomes a habit. CBT will help you inculcate good habits into your daily lifestyle, and you will become a better you.

Here are some guidelines that could help you, daily, to achieve your goals.

Pleasant Activity Scheduling

Pleasant activity scheduling is not as effective as behavioral therapy techniques but is particularly useful for those who are suffering from depression.

Try this: Write down the next 21 days on a piece of paper starting from today (Thursday, Friday, Saturday, etc.). For each day, schedule a pleasant activity—things that you love doing. It could be as easy as reading a chapter from a novel. An alternative method is to plan an activity for a day that will give you an edge and a sense of competence, accomplishment, and mastery. Also, pick something small that you wouldn't usually do—target anything that won't take you less than 10 minutes to accomplish. An improved method is to plan three nice activities every day; make it one in the morning, one at noon and the other one in the evening. Having events that bring high levels of positive emotions daily in your life will make you think less and be less negative.

Situation Exposure Hierarchies

Situation exposure hierarchy is doing things that you normally abstain from doing. For instance, an individual who has an eating disorder might have a list of forbidden foods, with ice cream topping the list and full-fat yogurt at the bottom. Someone who has social anxiety might decide that asking someone out on a date causes the highest anxiety, but asking someone for directions causes the least.

The idea of the hierarchy is to make a list of 10 items that cause the most anxiety or negative trigger, with 10 being the most. For example, for the eating disorder above, the ice cream would be 10 and the yogurt 1. The logic is to work your way up the list from the smallest to the highest—to expose yourself to these things in order to face your fears.

Imagery Based Exposure

A version of imagery exposure involves having a recent memory that provokes intense negative emotions. For example, a student of clinical psychology that was given a critical report by the supervisor—in imagery based exposure, the person might bring the scenario while the report was given to mind and remember vividly (example, what the room looked like, the tone the supervisor used).

They will also attempt to precisely label thoughts and emotions that they have experienced during interactions and what their urges are (example, to get angry or run out of the room to cry). In extended imagery exposure, the person will have to keep visualizing images until the level of discomfort is being reduced to half of its a starting point (say from 8/10 to 4/10).

Imagery based exposure can assist counter ruminations just because it assists in making intrusive, painful experiences that can likely trigger rumination, due to this, it also leads to a decrease in avoidance coping. When a person is not comfortable by the intrusive experiences gained, they will be able to choose healthier coping actions.

CBT Method

Setting realistic goals and understanding how to solve problems (e.g., engaging in more social tasks; learning how to be deciphered).

In some instances, CBT is most effective when it's done along with different remedies, including antidepressants or other drugs.

Also, fairly little is understood regarding the process of fitting treatments (such as CBT) to individuals. Skilled practitioners, though, are often ready to accommodate CBT to a vast array of circumstances and people.

Example 1

Jenny has been fighting with problematic drinking for decades. She understood there could be alcoholic beverages at the upcoming company party. She also knew her co-workers sometimes put a lot of pressure on her to drink. Jenny along with also her therapist developed a plan just before the party. Jenny chose to avoid the punch and only drink what she could cope with. She consumed soft drinks, possessed no more than one alcoholic beverage, stayed no longer than just three hours, and ask her boyfriend to pick her up after the party.

Example 2

John believed he had been "no good" and a "failure" in the office, in his romantic relationship as well as in his immediate environment. Through time, he came to realize bad stuff would take place and that things could always be problematic for him. This made him give up easily and believe there is "no point in striving."

John's therapist helped him identify all these beliefs and considered evidence for and from them. He discovered that he viewed the world in black and white, and commenced challenging himself to find the balance. John also figured out how to be more assertive and also perform activities that made him feel good about himself.

Cognitive Tools

Once individuals tackle the practices of self-monitoring and personal examination, they often uncover dysfunctional methods of thinking and problematic ways of thinking which prohibit them from success. If and when you locate these achievement banning mental routines, you can alter them using the practice of cognitive restructuring, or the practice of determining, hard, and altering unwanted thoughts into more prudent choices. The dysfunctional imagined record and ABCD version we touched above will steer you toward discovering and transforming success banning cognitions.

Behavioral Tools

While trying to transform dysfunctional methods of thinking and problematic habits of the head there's an excellent strategy. CBT therapists may often have to help their sufferers find and release limiting core beliefs observed below surface degree cognitions. As it's improbable to triumph without needing complete confidence in ourselves, letting go of these unwanted beliefs we hold about ourselves is equally vital for achievement. Luckily, we've come across evidence that no longer serves our demands from job behavioral exercises and tasks. Behavioral stimulation (climbing good reinforcement & decreasing unfavorable behavioral routines), behavioral rehearsal (training for impending occasions & situations), along with behavioral experiments (information-gathering exercises used to test the validity of thoughts & beliefs) are three common behavioral tools.

360-degree opinions

If you wish to improve your levels of social-emotional skills, your abilities to communicate with others, along with your professional standing, one effective instrument is 360-degree feedback or multisource opinions. While 360-degree evaluations are most frequently utilized in settings that are professional, they can also be useful to gauge others view us in societal, family, and community surroundings. By having others that you regularly interact with fill out a test assessment of one's weakness and strengths, you can acquire invaluable insight into the ways others view you personally and discover undeveloped skills which could help elevate you to the next level. It is critical not to become upset, as most of the feedback you receive needs to be accepted wholeheartedly and employed for expansion.

Values Clarification Exercise

The last tool we're going to look at that will be terrific for people struggling to locate meaning in existence is available from the shape of the popular Acceptance and Commitment Therapy clinic called the values caution practice. It's fairly easy to fault individual development with the faulty notion that success, money, and improved connections are the things we should be after. Reevaluate your values and determine the type of individual you wish to become. This may help steer you towards improving your levels of well-being.

Depending upon the verifiable efficacy of CBT, it is clear how all of us can utilize its orderly strategies to spiral towards the accomplishment of our goals. We could all achieve our goals by defining good results, building intelligent goals, committing to self-monitoring and self-evaluation, while also employing CBT techniques to help along the way.

Chapter 4: CBT Advantages and Methods

In the present society, health practitioners and psychiatrists are speedy to prescribe psychotropic drugs which often accompany dangerous negative side effects for any disorder that is due to idea patterns. But if you were told that there was a superior, more secure way to take care of and cure strain and mind disorders through cognitive behavioral therapy, would you try it?

CBT is just a form of psychotherapy which highlights the importance of inherent thoughts in ascertaining how we act and feel. CBT is regarded as one of the absolute most prosperous forms of psychotherapy to emerge in decades; CBT has become the focus of countless scientific tests.

CBT therapists discover, investigate, and transform their particular thought patterns, and reactions since they are what creates our senses and determines our behaviors. Using CBT therapy boosts patient's quality of life and also help them handle stress better compared to patients battling with tough situations independently.

What may surprise you about CBT as a core basic theory is that extreme scenarios, interactions with different people, and negative events are not usually accountable for our poor moods and problems. Instead, CBT therapists view precisely the opposite as being the cause. It's our reactions to events, the more things we tell ourselves in regards to these occasions—that can be within our control—that wind up affecting our quality of life. This is great news because it indicates we can modify ourselves.

Using cognitive behavioral therapy, we can learn to alter the way we feel, which in turn alters the way we see and cope with tough circumstances when they arise. We are now better at intercepting disruptive notions that cause us to be stressed, isolated, and depressed, and likely too mentally obese and reluctant to change negative habits. When we could accurately and calmly start looking at situations without distorting reality or incorporating limitations or fears, we will be able to understand just how to react appropriately to help us feel better in the long run in a means that creates us feel speediest in the very long run.

Here are a few benefits of cognitive behavioral therapy:

1. Lowers Symptoms of Depression

CBT is one of the most rapid, empirically supported treatments for depression. Studies demonstrate that CBT helps patients overcome signs of depression: such rage and low drive. It also lowers their risk of relapses in the future. CBT is thought to get the job done well. It's known for relieving depression because it delivers changes in cognition (feelings) that fuels vicious cycles of unwanted feelings along with rumination.

An analysis published in the journal, Cognitive Behavioral Therapy for Mood Disorders found that CBT is protective towards severe episodes of depression and can be utilized alongside or in place of anti-depressant drugs. CBT has also demonstrated promise as an approach for helping handle post-partum depression as well as an adjunct to drug treatment for bipolar patients.

Also, preventative cognitive therapy (a version of CBT) paired with anti-depressants were found to help patients that underwent long-term depression. Even the 2018 human study analyzed 289 members and afterward randomly assigned them to PCT and antidepressants, anti-depressants independently, or PCT with diminishing use of anti-depressants after healing. The study found that clinical therapy coupled together with antidepressant treatment was first-rate in comparison to alcoholism treatment alone.

1. Reduces Anxiety

There are strong indications that CBT could cure transmitted illnesses. Strong signs are seeing CBT cure for illnesses that are transmitted, such as panic disorders, obsessive-compulsive disorder, social anxiety disorder, generalized anxiety disorder, and post-traumatic stress disorder pressure disease. Overall, CBT shows both effectiveness in randomized controlled trials and efficacy in both naturalistic settings between patients with anxiety and therapists. Researchers have found that CBT functions well as an organic treatment for anxiety because it comprises various combinations of the following techniques:

Psycho-education regarding the character of fear and anxiety, self-monitoring of outward symptoms, bodily exercises, cognitive restructuring (by way of instance disconfirmation), the image along with in vivo experience of feared stimuli (exposure therapy), weaning from unsuccessful safety signals, along with relapse prevention.

1. Helps Deal with Eating Disorders

CBT has been proven to help significantly handle the underlying psychopathology of eating disorders and question the over-evaluation of shape and weight. Besides, it can interfere with the aid of sterile body weights, improve urge control, help prevent binge eating or purging, decrease feelings of isolation, and also support patients eventually become comfortable with "trigger food items" or situations using exposure therapy. Cognitive therapy is now the procedure of choice in treating bulimia nervosa and "eating disorders not otherwise defined" (ED-NOS) the two most popular eating disease diagnoses. There's also evidence it could assist in healing around sixty percent of people with anorexia, which is considered to be one of the most challenging mental illnesses to cure or prevent from failing.

1. Reduce Addictive Behaviors and Substance Abuse

Studies have shown that CBT is excellent in supporting cannabis and other drug dependencies, such as alcohol and opioid addiction. It also helps people quit smoking tobacco and gambling. Studies published in the Oxford Journal of Medicine Public Health concerning solutions for smoking cessation have also found that working skills realized during CBT periods were tremendously helpful in cutting relapses in cigarette quitters and it appears to be superior to other curative approaches. There is also stronger support for CBT's behavioral procedures (assisting to stop impulses) at the treatment of problematic gaming addictions in comparison to control remedies.

1. Helps Improve Self-Esteem and Assurance

Even if you never suffer from any significant mental problems in any respect, CBT can assist you in replacing harmful, negative thoughts that cause low self-esteem, with positive affirmations and expectations. This helps open new tactics to handle stress, improve relationships, and increase the drive to try new issues.

1. Helps you become more rational

The brain essentially acts as a neutral object, giving a response based on the information at its disposal and also the way it was trained to respond. Cognitive therapy trains the brain to act rationally.

In CBT, it is believed that our thoughts lead to how we feel, behave and handle situations. The good thing about this is that we have a chance to change how we think and act right even if the situation remains unchanged.

CBT helps patients to control the thinking pattern that leads to irrational behaviors. Those undergoing CBT treatment are thought strategies with which they can cope better whenever automatic negative thoughts (ANTs) arise. CBT helps to develop ways to control the brain.

1. It boosts your self-belief

CBT helps to boost your self-confidence and works on your belief system, so you gain much better control of your thoughts. With self-confidence, you will be able to face any challenge that comes your way to achieving success and attaining your goals.

1. It helps you stay calm and relaxed

The initial stage of learning about social anxiety therapy is to devise a new way to anxiety response. With CBT treatment one won't be frightened by anxiety or anything that happens abruptly as we approach things with much peace and calmness. It teaches one best way to handle different kinds of situations that may arise in a more relaxed manner.

1. CBT helps to raise your expectations as you expect better outcomes

Due to our prior history and self-doubts, we often expect negative things to happen to us. We are always expecting things to turn out bad for us. CBT works on those thoughts and your belief system so that you can start acting more rational. As our thoughts and action become more rational, our expectations also turn out to be more logical as expert positive things to happen.

With CBT, we are made to repeatedly question ourselves to ascertain if our old beliefs are rational or not. Are they fact-based? Alternatively, are they things that have been our norm for years, and we have never questioned it? What is the real truth?

Do we pay attention to feedback from others or do we only pay attention to our internal negative conclusions? Is there any chance that we've fallen into the trap of self-brainwashing over the years?

Our own old automatic negative thoughts can reprocess throughout the brain. Have you found a way to stop them? Have you explored the possible explanation for your actions and have you thought about it that there might be no justifiable reason to feel fearful and anxious?

As our belief system is transformed by our thoughts and beliefs which bring about physical changes in the brain. An improved way of thinking leads us to expect a different outcome, a positive one. Your outcome depends on what you think about the outcome.

Other benefits of cognitive behavioral therapy include:

- Preventing the relapse of an addiction
- Resolving issues in relationships
- Recognizing negative thoughts and emotions
- Chronic pain management
- Anger Management
- Ability to coping with grief and loss
- Dealing with sleep disorders

How Cognitive Behavior Therapy Works

CBT operates by pinpointing thoughts that continuously arise using them as signs for favorable activity and substituting them with healthy, and far more empowering alternatives.

The heart of CBT is mastering self-coping techniques, offering individuals the ability to handle their reactions/responses of situations logically, alter the thoughts they tell themselves, and exercise "logical self-counseling." While this helps the CBT therapist/counselor and affected person build confidence and possess a great romantic relationship, the power lies in the individual's control. How willing a patient is ready to explore her or his thoughts, be open-minded, complete research assignments and clinic patience throughout the CBT course of action, can all determine how favorable CBT will be for these.

Features that make CBT an Effective Tool

Pragmatic method

CBT techniques and theory are predicated on rational thinking, which means they aim to spot and use these details. Even the "inductive technique" of CBT encourages individuals to examine their own beliefs and perceptions to see whether they are realistic. With CBT, there is an inherent premise that many behavioral and psychological responses are all learned.

With CBT therapists' help, patients realize that their long-held premises and hypotheses are partially wrong, which reduces unnecessary anxiety and suffering.

Feeling difficult or debilitating emotions: Most CBT therapists can help individuals learn to remain calm and clear-headed even if they are faced with unwanted scenarios. Learning to accept difficult feelings as "part of life" is crucial, and it can help prevent one from developing a bad habit. Usually, we become upset about our strong feelings and become more distressed. Instead of adding self-blame, rage, despair, or disappointment to already-tough feelings, CBT instructs sufferers to calmly accept a problem without making it even worse.

Questioning and expressing

Cognitive behavioral therapists typically ask patients lots of questions to help them gain a fresh and realistic perspective about the problem and also assist them to control how they feel.

Definite Agendas and Techniques

CBT is usually done in a succession of sessions that all possess a particular objective, concept, or technique that work together. Unlike a few other types of therapy, sessions are not exclusively for the therapist and individual to speak openly without an agenda on your mind. CBT therapists teach their customers the way to handle challenging thoughts and feelings by practicing particular techniques during sessions which may, later on, be implemented into life when they're most wanted.

Cognitive Behavioral Therapy vs. Other Types of Psychotherapy

CBT can be a sort of psychotherapy, which means that it calls for open discussion between patient and therapist. You may know about several other forms of psychotherapy and you're wondering what makes CBT stand out. Sometimes when there is an overlap between several types of psychotherapy, a therapist could use techniques from various psychotherapy approaches to assist patients in attaining their goals. For example, to help anyone with a phobia, CBT may be coupled together with exposure therapy.

How is CBT different From Other Popular Forms of Therapy?

The National Alliance on Mental Illness states how CBT Is Different from other popular forms of therapy:

CBT vs. Dialectical Behavior Therapy (DBT)

CBT and DBT and are most likely the most comparable curative approaches; nevertheless DBT depends heavily on validation or accepting uncomfortable thoughts, feelings, and behaviors. DBT therapists help individuals detect balance between acceptance and change from using applications like mindfulness guided meditation.

CBT vs. Exposure Therapy

Exposure therapy is a sort of cognitive behavioral therapy that's often utilized to treat eating disorders, phobias, and anti-inflammatory disease. It teaches individuals to practice calming strategies and little series of "exposures" to triggers (issues which are most dreaded) to become less concerned with the outcome.

CBT vs. Interpersonal Therapy

Social therapy concentrates on the relationships a patient has together with his or her family, friends, and co-workers. Focusing on societal interactions and recognizing negative patterns such as isolation, jealousy, blame, or aggression are part of therapy. CBT can be employed with social therapy to help reveal subjective beliefs and notions forcing negative behavior and supporting the others.

CBT Journal work

Journal work is the most important part of CBT; this might help you;

- Practice balanced and accurate self-talk.

- Learn how to change and control aberrations and thoughts.

- Use self-examinations to reflect and respond in healthy and better ways.

- Learn how you can properly comprehend and precisely assess emotional behaviors such as external situations and reactions.

- Through utilizing different methods it's possible to learn how you can live well and balanced with both your mind and body.

Once more, the duration of time a person spends in treatment is usually less compared to some other therapy. Also, note that CBT will not *cure* depression or other issues, but rather you will get measurable relief while improving your daily life.

Chapter 5: Disorders, Medical, and Emotional Issues CBT is Expected to Treat

CBT can be very useful for a lot of disorders, medical, and emotional problems. Some of the common ones will be discussed in detail in subsequent chapters. Here is a brief overview of some disorders you should expect CBT to treat.

Panic Disorders

CBT assists in targeting panic disorder by bringing the client to what he/she fears most, these exposure periods assist every individual in learning that they could also experience symptoms of being aroused without having to fear what comes next. Interceptive exercise gives room for every individual to face the sensations they get physically that comes along with panic. Example, Hyperventilation or bodily spinning can also be introduced during sessions to help induce lightheadedness or feelings of dizziness. With imaginary exposures, the therapist reads scripts that focus on an individual's fears during the sessions over and over again until there is a feeling that the personal fears have reduced to some extent.

With Vivo Exposure, the individual's fears can be drastically reduced, allowing them to avoid situations that might cause a panic attack. On certain occasions, there are groups of challenging problems that are brought about, and that individual follows the steps with the aid of the therapist. Afterwards, the individual's attitude will change, allowing them to consistently seek out and face every hard situation.

Depression

CBT can also help depression by using a known technique which is also known as behavior activation. Using the behavior activation, both the therapist and client work together to introduce new events that are pleasant to the individual's life. This will help to change the mood of that individual by avoiding the reverse, increasing self-confidence, increasing the level of usefulness, physical activity, and ultimately reducing negative thoughts. Behavior activation contains many different behaviors, the ones that are most common are the ones that bring out more pleasant activities, and other behaviors that will stress out the individuals like cleaning a messy apartment, calling alienated family members, or filing taxes.

Attention Deficit/Hyperactivity Disorder (ADHD)

Under normal conditions, treatment for the first line of ADHD is medications (psychostimulants). Most times, only medications aren't enough for many people who have ADHD. CBT for ADHD aims to assists many individuals in changing coping skills to handle their symptoms and deal with functional and emotional effects that comes with people living with the disorder. Patients are always encouraged to give real-life examples of some specific issues and difficulties they face with the therapist to help find the best solution. It is also important that the therapist and patient introduce some problems that might end up arising and make plans that will help solve them.

Obsessive Compulsive Disorder (OCD)

The preferred method for today's treatment for OCD is weekly CBT treatment that usually involves (exposure and response/ritual prevention) ERP exercise. Exposure and response prevention connote that the first individual introduces themselves to thoughts, objects, images, and situations that make them anxious or obsessed (exposure). Individuals then oppose doing a compulsive behavior when the obsessions or anxiety is triggered that is response prevention. This helps stop or reduce compulsions.

Social Phobia/Social Anxiety

The therapist that uses CBT to assist clients in getting a new way of behaving and thinking by adopting realistic and positive thoughts to change all bad and unrealistic thoughts. Cognitive restructuring is necessary for those individuals that are faced with societal anxiety, as they are learning to question and challenge every truth behind their beliefs. This can be done by giving solid evidence against every other belief that is problematic in a Socratic conversation. Behavioral experiments are also important as they show individuals that disastrous events known by irrational beliefs don't always end up happening during the periods of exposure exercises. This helps explain lies about their beliefs.

Bipolar Disorder

Certainly, most of the patients that are suffering from Bipolar disorder are being given medications, most of the time mood stabilizers, and initial evidence explains to us that CBT is an effective therapy to pharmacotherapy. CBT for Bipolar disorder exerts more force on mood regulations and psycho-education. Psycho-education helps to educate individuals on what the illness is all about and the consequences, their side effects, medication options, symptoms, as well as the early warning signs of episodes. CBT helps individuals to track and also identify their mood swings and decrease emotional reactivity through mindful exercise, breathing, or self-soothing (distractions).

Generalized Anxiety Disorder (GAD)

CBT is very effective in treating GAD; it helps decrease not just the actual symptoms of anxiety, but also what is associated with depressive symptoms, which will improve quality of life. One of the most effective trainings for GAD is what is known as relaxation training. During sessions, individuals must learn how to reduce the tension in the muscle and shallow breathing, as they are both known to cause anxiety and stress. The two strategies that are commonly used in CBT are paced respiration, which involves being aware of reducing your breath and progressive muscle relaxation which systematically involves tension and relaxation of different muscle groups. There are other useful relaxation methods that can be used which include; meditation, listening to music, massage, and yoga.

Schizophrenia

CBT has now been recommended as a treatment to be used for schizophrenia, it can be used alongside medications. Using CBT, the individuals get to know that there is a link that connects their feelings and patterns of thinking that underlies their discomfort. It also focuses on disputing and identifying the client's irrational beliefs through behavioral experiments and certain discoveries.

CBT can be useful in helping the clients in every aspect so they can validate their beliefs. These kinds of experiment usually encourage clients to be active which eventually leads to a deeper level understanding.

Bulimia Nervosa

CBT is the most used treatment procedure for bulimia; the illness at its core has concerns with the shape of the body and weight, which leads to excessive dieting and behaviors that are controlled by body image.

Excessive dieting also makes one susceptible to rapid eating; CBT treatment focuses on improving the motivation to change, change dieting to a flexible and regular one, and reduce your concerns about weight, preventing relapse and body shape. CBT has also shown to be more efficient and acceptable antidepressant medications in destroying excessive eating, CBT is expected to remove excess eating and purging in almost 30-50% cases and this decreases the level of other psychiatric symptoms and improves social functioning and self-esteem.

Fear of Flying/Flying phobia

CBT is also very effective for the treatment of many phobias, the flight phobia is a very common complaint that CBT can efficiently treat. Psycho-education is one of the most important components used in CBT treatment, and this is usually added with cognitive training and relaxation techniques. Imaginal exposure is also very useful; it can assist clients in thinking about situations where the clients are on a plane, or any other circumstance that might help induce fear, this will try to raise their anxiety over a short period. However, once they are thinking about the same thing over and over again, their anxiousness decreases each time and this will help them handle much deeper real-life situations much better. Recent development in treating the phobia of flying is reality exposure where individuals are exposed to their fears in a 3D computer-compilation. This will help create a real-life environment, the same principle of being exposed technically works the same.

There are several other disorders that CBT can be used for; we will also discuss some of them in details in the ensuing chapters.

Chapter 6: CBT for Depression

Life could be funny at times; and sometimes, you feel like you are down. When you are down or you think that life is against you is what every other person feels in today's world. Over 14.8 million adults in the US are affected by a Major Depressive Disorder according to the Anxiety and Depression Association of America.

Depression can be serious as it gives room for a "normal" functioning difficulty which means so much that you simply get through the day by totally being overwhelmed, and then you can turn to alcohols and drugs for more comfort. When you are down, it is like the world is crashing down, just know that there is a way out and there is no need for you to keep suffering.

CBT for depression starts with placing greater attention on reducing the symptoms of depression through cognitive and behavioral techniques intended to detect and challenge harmful automatic thoughts.

Once there has been a significant reduction in the symptom of depression, individuals practicing CBT may then be able to focus on how they can prevent future occurrence.

Cognitive Behavioral therapy for people who are depressed can help restore the zeal you have for the world we are living in; it can assist you in thinking in a more healthy way, help to prevail over an addiction. Before going into details of what CBT is, and how it can help to treat depression, though, it is very important to know the primary types of depression.

Types of Depression

Persistent Depressive Disorder (PDD)

This is also formerly known as dysthymia; it is a type of depression that most times continues for two years. Generally, this is much more severe than even major depression, but you will experience similar symptoms. PDD also shows itself as stress, inability to enjoy life, and irritability.

Major Depression

This involves suffering from depressive symptoms (5 or more) for about two weeks; major depressive episodes are disabling. It might interfere with the ability for you to work, sleep, eat, and study. These kinds of episodes only happen for a few periods throughout your lifetime, after a terrible experience like the demise of a family member or the downfall of any relationship.

Bipolar Depression

This type of depressive disorder shows when your life is in a period of shifting mood cycles that includes harsh or gentle high (hypomania or mania) depressive lows and crushing.

Now you are already aware of the major types of depression disorders, how common it might be, the symptoms; it is good to know that there is an effective treatment for depression. CBT is one of the types of psychotherapy that changes your thought pattern; it also assists in changing your moods and behaviors. The therapy originates from the work of Aaron T.Beck and Albert Ellis in 1950-1960s. Generally speaking, CBD is a treatment for depression that blends cognitive and behavioral therapy in which the therapist assists in identifying a particular bad pattern, and your behaviors response to stress, and challenging circumstances.

Signs and Symptoms of Depression

If you have a concern about depression, ask yourself these questions whether you will be able to identify with any of the following symptoms:

- Lack of interest in things you usually enjoy

- Uncontrollable negative thoughts

- Irritability, short-tempered, and aggression

- Engaging in reckless behavior

- Feelings of helplessness and hopelessness

- Appetite changes, such as eating far less or too much

- Self-loathing; a feeling of being worthless and guilty

- Using illegal or prescription drugs in excess

- Unnatural tiredness

- Drinking more alcohol than usual

- Unexplained pains and aches which also includes stomach pains, back pains, sore muscles, and headaches.

If you answer to any or more of these, you might be depressed, and Cognitive Behavioral therapy might be able to help.

Going for a CBT depression can be discouraging. However, here is a little guide of what will be involved, so be prepared:

Therapy

You may want to meet with your therapist for a period of 5 to 20 weekly or biweekly periods. In general, periods might last between 30 to 60 minutes, all through the beginning of 2-4 sessions; your therapist will know if you are truly right for the treatment or whether you are comfortable with it. A therapist can ask about your background or your past, CBT also focuses on what the present is all about, but at times, it can be imperative to open up about your past and how it affects you presently. You decide what exactly you need and how well you want to deal with it, along with your therapist.

The work

With the support of your therapist, each problem you have is broken down into different parts. To help you with that, you might be asked to keep a diary to assist you in identifying every one of your emotions, personal ways, and physical feelings. Both of you take a look at the behaviors, thoughts, and feelings to see how they are affecting each other and how they might also affect you. If they are not realistic or helpful; your therapist might figure out a way to change any negativity. The therapist might also give you "assignments" which involves practicing how to identify changes you will need to make every day in your life. During the time of every meeting, you will have more opportunities to talk about your progress since the last meeting; if there is a specific duty that is not working out for you, you should discuss such issues. You might never be able to do things that you love to do; you might also dictate the pace of your therapy and can also keep developing your skills when the sessions are complete. This will allow you to remain happy for many years to come.

How Does Cognitive Behavioral Therapy (CBT) Differ From Other Depression Treatments?

The method and general focus of Cognitive Behavioral Therapy is kind of different from many other, more traditional depression treatments. For instance, Cognitive Behavioral Therapy: Modifies behaviors in the immediate present while changing your thought patterns.

CBT majorly addresses your problematic thinking and undesirable behaviors.

- Clear goals are fixed for each session and the long-term. i.e., Goal-oriented.

- CBT is educational. You monitor your thoughts and feelings, and then you commit these to paper. The therapist will also teach you essential coping skills, such as problem-solving.

- Makes you play an active part in your learning and recovery. You will also be able to complete "homework" assignments that are reviewed at the beginning of the next session.

- CBT employs multiple strategies, including role-playing, guided discovery and behavioral experiments.

- CBT is time limited.

How Cognitive Behavioral Therapy Can Help With Depression

We are all aware of how debilitating depression can be. Depression is an extremely common condition. The illness impacts your life negatively as well as the lives of your family and friends. It can go a long way to affect your employers and co-workers.

Depression has impacted negatively on the general functioning of the society as a whole. For example, it is a fact that the illness imposes a financial burden on you, the sufferer, as well as on your family, caregiver, your employer, and insurance provider.

CBT can guarantee a new lease on life if you're going through depression. Conversely, if you have severe major depression, CBT, delivered in conjunction with other medication, is a very effective or efficient treatment.

Thinking negatively can slow depression recovery, and the reason is self-evident: If you have negative thoughts, you're more likely to stay depressed. But what is less obvious is the way people with depression deal with their positive emotions. Researchers have made an astounding observation: People with depression never lack positive emotions; they will never allow themselves to feel them.

This cognitive style is known as "dampening," and it involves suppressing positive emotions with thoughts such as, "This good feeling won't last." "I don't deserve to be this happy." For example, a new mom with postpartum depression might begin to doubt herself and ability to recover because she's a bad mother for being depressed in the first place.

Defensive pessimism makes people with depression think this way. It seeks to protect against getting high hopes dashed. "You never want to be the fool, so you resort to dampening positive thoughts to protect yourself from potential disappointment."

CBT is believed to help significantly with depression treatment. With CBT, you and your therapist work hand to hand, i.e., together, to reach an agreement on behavior patterns that need to be changed. The purpose or goal is to recalibrate the part of your brain that's keeping such a tight hold on happy thoughts.

An unanticipated reaction to a major life events might be at the root of the dampening effect. Through CBT, you and your therapist address it and work toward putting it into perspective.

Regular Cognitive Behavior therapy sessions and work people do on there can help to reinforce the new patterns. Recognizing those negative thoughts and leaving them behind can be very liberating.

Cognitive Behavioral Therapy Techniques to Counteract the Negative Thinking of Depression

People with depression don't respond well to self-study. For this reason, it's recommended to commit to CBT for at least seven weeks. Your therapist will teach you strategies that can help frustrate or counteract the negative thinking associated with depression. He or she can also help you stay on track with practicing the techniques.

Here is the list of CBT strategies you might work on with your therapist:

1. Locate the problem and brainstorm or investigate solutions.

Talking and Journaling with your therapist can help you discover the root of your depression. Once you have any idea or impression, write down what's bothering you and think of ways to improve the situation.

A hallmark of depression is hopelessness — not believing that things can ever get better. Write down lists of things that can be done to improve a situation and it will help to ease depressive feelings. For instance, if you're battling loneliness, action steps may involve joining a local club in line with your interests or signing up for dating online.

1. Write self-statements to counteract negative thoughts.

After finding the root problems of your depression, think of all the negative thoughts you use to dampen positive ones. Write a self-statement to counteract with each negative thought. Always note your self-statements and repeat them back to yourself when you notice the little voice in your head creeping in to snuff out a positive thought. Soon enough, you'll create new associations, replacing all the negative thoughts with positive ones.

1. Self-affirmations shouldn't be overly positive or else the mind might find it difficult to accept it.

For instance, if the negative thought says, "I feel so depressed right now," instead of saying, "I'm feeling really happy now," it could be better rephrased as, "Every life experience ups and downs, and mine does, too." This tells you that it's okay to bump up the degree or rate of happiness you experience. At the same time, one's mind applauds itself for keeping joy and happiness in check to protect from disappointment. It's very good to recognize that part of you that's trying to do something healthy.

At some point, self-statements become too routine and need to be refreshed. Rephrase your self-statements or translate it into any lan-

EMOTIONAL INTELLIGENCE AND COGNITIVE BEHAVIORAL THERAPY

guage that you speak, perhaps it could spring up your happy feelings a bit. For instance, the self-statement, "It's very good to explore my ups" might become "It's good to have a very super 'up' day."

If you have a partner or loved one suffering from depression, there is a possibility that CBT will effectively treat them depending on the severity. Also, you might face the challenge about your loved one feeling reluctant to seek help for depression.

The ideal way to raise such person's spirits toward going for CBT session is to calmly discuss their fears and concerns about going for the session, instead of telling them they have to go. Show concern and support and reassure them that you don't think something is wrong with them; instead, you only want them to get some help to cope with their present challenge.

Sometimes, depressed people want help but don't have an idea about what to do and where to start. By offering to assist in visiting a therapist to schedule an appointment can improve their chances of committing to CBT.

Chapter 7: CBT for Anxiety

CBT is mostly used everywhere as therapy for anxiety disorders; many researches have been undergone to show that the effectiveness of this treatment of phobia's, generalized disorders, and panic disorder among so many other likely conditions. This examines the terrible patterns and aberrations in the way we view things like the world and ourselves generally, just as the name implies, it involves two categories;

1. **Behavior Therapy:** This looks deeply into how you can react and behave in circumstances that bring about anxiety.
2. **Cognitive Therapy:** This observes how bad thoughts or cognitions add to the anxiety.

The fundamental proposition of CBT is that our thoughts and not what happens externally affect how we are feeling, i.e., not exactly the circumstance that you are feeling right now that determines the perception of that particular situation. Example, Let's just say that you have been invited somewhere for a party. Let's look at how well you have different ways of viewing the invitation and how this thought can affect your emotional state.

Situation 1: A friend gives you an invitation to a big party

Thought A: The party sounds like there will be lots of fun, I'm excited to get out and meet new people.

Emotions: Tranquility, excitement.

Thoughts B: Parties are not my kind of thing, I prefer to stay in and watch movies.

Emotions: Neutral.

Thoughts C: I do not know what to say or how to act when I am at a party, I will probably make a fool of myself if I go.

Emotions: Unhappy, Anxious.

Now you know that one type of event can turn out different for people with different types of emotions. It all strongly depends on every individuals' expectations, beliefs, and attitude. For this type of people with anxiety disorders, terrible patterns of thinking evoke the terrible beliefs and thoughts. This conception is brought about when you change your way you think, and you can also change the way you feel.

Cognitive Behavioral Techniques you will need to beat anxiety

1. The Ability to Recognize Rumination

Rumination is when you are bothered over and over again by a worrisome thought when you think about issues; it lowers your capacity to solve any problems. If you are constantly ruminating, it is best to patiently wait to solve the problem first until when you discover that the problem has gone beyond the issue of solving and then begin to ruminate over it.

If you can learn to recognize when you are ruminating, then it is proper for you to use Cognitive Behavioral methods or being mindful to assist you in stopping the act of ruminating. The right thing to do when ruminating is to accept that you are having whatsoever thought you have right now, know that you might not be accurate, but it allows those thoughts to quickly pass in their own time instead of blocking it away.

1. The Ability and Willingness to use Mindful Techniques

Mindful techniques also assist in decreasing anxiety and then raising your willpower, practicing being mindful will assist you in reducing avoidance, make other better choice even when the feelings are anxious, and this will help you reduce rumination. Try the 10-minute mindful walking exercise.

1. The Ability to Tolerate Uncertainty

Research has made it known that not enduring uncertainty is one of the significant factors in anxiety and being depressed. Not enduring uncertainty is having anxiety and when you are not 100% sure that a negative event will not happen. People who are not able to tolerate uncertainties often keep away from situations like reassurance seek, delay taking action, refusing to delegate, do excessive checking and procrastination.

1. Ability to Recognize Thoughts Distortions

Different types of thought aberrations include lowering your own personal ability to cope, personalized mind reading, being judgmental about other people or yourself, making too much of a negative forecast, every other person as white or black instead of gray, entitlement thoughts (example, thinking about the normal rules that should not apply) and many more. The major key is to know that thought aberration is to question yourself whenever you have the feelings of depression. You can also try doing a CBT Thought Record.

1. The Ability to Talk to Yourself, Kindly about your Imperfections and Mistakes

Criticizing yourself when you try something and make a mistake, or when your imperfections show up can likely lead to rumination and avoid coping. Studies have shown us that when you talk to yourself, it does not just make you feel better but also increase your self-esteem and improves motivation.

Thoughts challenging in CBT for anxiety

The cognitive restructuring is also known as thought challenging is a series of steps that help to confront the bad thinking ways that most of the time contributes to your anxiety and then change them with more realistic, positive thoughts. This takes about three steps;

- Replacing Negative Thoughts with Realistic Thoughts

Once you know the irrational and negative aberrations in your thoughts, you can then change them with fresh and positive thoughts. Your therapist can devise a calming and realistic statement that you can always tell yourself when you are preventing or facing a circumstance that increases your anxiety level.

- Identifying your Negative Thoughts

With anxiety disorders, some situations are known to be very deadly than they are known to be, to someone with a phobia for germs, shaking someone's else hands may seem threatening. Although it might be possible for you to see that it's an irrational fear, knowing your personal irrational, fearful thoughts can be very hard. One way is to question yourself about what you are thinking about when you are anxious. Your personal therapist can assist you with this process.

- Challenging your Negative Thoughts

Using this method, your therapist can help you acquire how to examine anxiety-provoking thoughts; this also involves asking about the facts for your threatening thoughts, testing out the truth about the negative forecast, and analyzing beliefs that are not helping. Methods used for challenging negative thoughts involves weighing the pros and cons of worrying, conducting experiments, or keeping away from the things that you fear and know the realistic chance that you have been anxious about will suddenly happen.

To know how these challenging thoughts work during CCBT, understand the following example; Maria will not take the subway just because she is scared she might pass out and then people might think she is actually crazy. Her therapist told her to jot down her terrible thoughts, the cognitive aberrations, or identifying what the error is in whatever she thinks about and then come up with an interpretation that is rational. The outcomes are stated below;

Challenging Negative Thoughts
Negative thought A: What if I pass out in the subway?
Cognitive aberrations: Forecast the worst.
More realistic thoughts: I have never passed out before, so it is not certain that I will.
Negative thought B: Once I pass out, it is going to be bad.
Cognitive aberration: Blowing things out of proportion
More Realistic Thoughts: If I pass out, I come around in a few minutes. That will be so terrible.
Negative thoughts C: People might assume that I am crazy
Cognitive Aberrations: Jump to conclusions
More realistic thoughts: People are most likely to be more concerned if I am okay.

Change negative thoughts with more represented one is much easier than done. Often, bad thoughts are part of lifelong ways of thinking; it involves doing extra work to break that habit. That is one of the reasons why CBT involves you practicing alone and at home too. CBT also involves;

- Confronting your fears (either in real life or imaginary).

- Learn to know when you are already feeling anxious and what that feels like in the body.

- Learn to cope with skills and relaxation methods to counteract pain and anxiety.

Exposure Therapy for Anxiety

Anxiety is not a favorable experience, so it is best naturally to keep away if you can, one of the methods that most people use is by staying clear of those problems that make them feel anxious. If you have fears for heights, you might try to drive hours out of your way to avoid crossing a very tall bridge, or if the fear of public speaking gets your stomach in knots, you might as well skip your best friend's wedding just to avoid making a toast. Aside from the fact that it might not be convenient, you will not have the opportunity of overcoming them.

Exposure therapy, as the name, implies that vulnerability to circumstances or objects that you tend to fear, the conception is that through consistent vulnerability, you will be able to feel a soaring control sense over every circumstance and then the anxiety begins to reduce. The exposure can be done in any of the two ways; you might want to imagine a scary problem for you to face a real-life situation. Exposure therapy might be used alone, or it might be used as part of the conducted CBT.

Systematic Desensitization

Instead of facing your greatest fear immediately, which can be used in exposure therapy, traumatizing which usually begins with problems that are only gentle threatening and this works up from there. This stepwise method is also known as systematic desensitization allows you to gradually replace your confidence, challenge your fears, and master skills to influence his panic.

Facing the fear of flying
Step A: Check out the photos of planes
Step B: Watch videos of planes on a flight

Step C: Watch how real planes take off
Step D: Book a plane ticket
Step E: Pack for your flight
Step F: Drive to airport
Step G: Check-in for your flight
Step H: Wait to board
Step I: Get on the plane
Step J: Take the flight.
Systematic desensitization involves three parts;

Learning Relaxation Skills

First of all, your personal therapist will explain to you a relaxation method which includes deep breathing or muscle relaxation which you can practice alone at home or in the therapy. Immediately, you start facing your fears, and this relaxation method will assist you in decreasing your physical anxiety response (like hyperventilating and trembling) also to encourage relaxation.

Creating a Step-By-Step List

The next agenda is to create a list of 10-20 scary circumstances that might increase your final goal, example, if one of your final goals is to face your fear of flying, you could solve this by simply taking a look at photos of planes and ending it with an actual flight. Each step should be as actual practical as possible, with a measurable and clear objective.

Working Through the Steps

Under the process of your therapist, you will start to work through the list to stay in each scary circumstance until your fears are gone, that way you will learn to know that your feelings might not hurt you and they will not leave, every time anxiety gets too extreme, you will learn to move to the relaxation technique that is learned. Immediately, you have been relaxed again, you can turn the attention back to the situation, in this way, you will work through the methods till you have been able to finish every step without feeling totally discomforted.

Complementary Therapies for Anxiety Disorder

As you begin to examine your personal anxiety disorder in therapy, you might also want to fully experiment with other complementary therapies that are intended to bring down your stress level by assisting you in achieving balance emotionally.

- Relaxation methods such as medication that is mindful, progressive muscle relaxation that can be regularly practiced and can decrease anxiety, increase your emotional well-being.

- Hypnosis can be sometimes used together with CBT for anxiety even when you are in a state of constant, profound relaxation; hypnotherapist uses various therapeutic methods to assist you in confronting your fears and looking at them from another angle.

- Exercise is one of the natural anxiety relievers and also increase stress, research has made it known that even a little period of exercise for about 30 minutes 3-5 times in a week can also provide better relief for anxiety. To achieve a better result, a maximum of an hour of exercise will do on most occasions.

- Biofeedback makes use of sensors that aid specific physiological functions like breathing, muscle tension, and heart rate which is used to explain to you how your body responds to anxiety and learn to control it using relaxation methods.

Making Anxiety Therapy Work for You

You cannot quickly rush to fix anxiety disorders, to overcome anxiety really takes being committed to it, and also take lots of time. Therapy also includes confronting your fears rather than staying away from them, at times, most people feel worse even before they get better. The most necessary thing is to get used to treatment and follow the advice that is given to you by your therapist. If you are discouraged with the way at which you are recovering, just keep it in the back of your mind that the therapy given for anxiety is always very efficient, and you will surely get the gains if you are able to see it through.

You can also give full support to your own anxiety therapist by always making good choices, everything you do from your level of activities to your life socially affects how anxious you become. Always set the pace for success by making an effort to allow relaxation, positive mental outlook and even vitality in your life daily.

- Adopt a lifestyle that is healthy, physical activities when done totally reduces anxiety and tension, so you should create time for regular exercises. Make sure you do not use drugs or alcohols to work with the symptoms and try to keep away from stimulants like nicotine or caffeine which allows for anxiety disorders to worsen.

- Learn about anxiety: For you to be able to overcome anxiety, it is very important that you learn to know where the problem lies and that is really where education lies, just know that only education will not completely cure an anxiety disorder, but it will assist you in getting more out of the therapy.

- Totally reduce stress in your life, and try to observe your life during stress, and look for methods to reduce it. Keep away from people who are always making you anxious and bluntly disagree on every responsibility, make extra time to have fun and have add relaxation to your daily schedule.

EMOTIONAL INTELLIGENCE AND COGNITIVE BEHAVIORAL THERAPY

- Cultivate having the right connections with every other person, being lonely and isolation makes it very easy to become anxious. Reduce your exposure by reaching out to people, make it important to see your friends, join support groups and share your concerns and worries with your loved ones.

Chapter 8: CBT for Fear and Phobias

Certain people immediately form a negative mindset against others rather than encouraging themselves to get to know positive things about other people.

Buddying up with other person working on the same methods with you and your friends can be very exciting whenever you have a positive mind and experiences that you are sharing every day. Here are few ways to use CBT to eliminate fear and phobia.

1. Accept disappointment as a common part of life

Some unexpected circumstance is an aspect of life and how well you respond to it shows how quickly you will move forward. Some people might just be going through break up, and then begin to blame themselves for what happened. Thoughts such as "what good is it to look good? I will never meet someone else like him/her," is an example.

Action plan:
Try as much as possible to know that those scenarios can be out of your control

Work on those things that are within your reach write down the things that happened, the experience gained from it and things you hope you will be able to do differently another time, watch for bad thoughts always coming to your minds. This will guide you on how to move on and feel good about it.

1. End each day by visualizing the best part

When the day is over, note down or type into a journal the things in your life that you are always grateful for, record every positive thought.

You could even share your thought online; this will help you find new friends or show you better ways to do things.

Treatment for Phobias

Phobias do not need to be treated until their fear is preventing them from performing the necessary task, working or having good relationships. Example, if you decide to live in the United States and you know that you have fears of tigers, you could decide not to visit the zoo; rather, you should spend more time learning how to treat your phobias. Most types of anxiety disorders have cures; showing that not all single treatment can work for all type of phobia. When you are looking for the treatment for a particular type of phobia, the methods each therapist might use may differ. Here are some common forms of therapy to treat phobias.

Cognitive Behavioral Therapies for Phobia's

Cognitive Behavioral Therapy (CBT) allows you to take charge of your fears by helping you gradually to change the way you think; its fundamental basis is the connections between thoughts, behaviors, and beliefs. A person who has phobia knows that his or her feared circumstances are really dangerous. It will then lead such person to develop negative thoughts as soon as such fear is faced. This might lead to several patterns to change his or her thoughts.

To successfully overcome this, the therapist might be needed first to develop a treatment plan. For instance, if you have a fear of dogs the treatment plan could be first to take out time to read all about dogs to watching movies about dogs. Also, take such person to a place where dogs are being taken care of to show that they are not harmful.

Group Therapies to Ease Fears

Cognitive Behavior theory is a very common type of groups that make up the phobia therapy, although, there are various forms of therapy to be used in this method. Some CBT sessions for phobia might be in the form of a seminar which may last for 1 hour or several days. For instance, those with the phobia of height or flying can assemble at the airport hotel for a brief meeting during the weekend. In this meeting, they will be able to engage themselves in combinations of vulnerability sessions and psych educational class within the airport.

Individual Therapy

Individual therapy makes it possible for the therapist and the individual to focus properly on each other, building a solid friendship and helping to work together to solve the issue. However, related therapies and psychoanalysis might progress for months or even many years while short-term therapies like CBT can produce results in just very few sessions.

Family Therapy

If the therapist discovers that the family could also contribute to the development of having phobias, it is possible to suggest the family as part of the therapy plans. A very common example is the application of the family therapy which allows for communications between other family members. Family therapy is a very common plan for children that have phobias.

Chapter 9: CBT for Maladaptive or Bad Habits

Maladaptive Behaviors refers to those behaviors that refrain your ability to improve to specific healthy situations. They prevent you from coping with the demands and stress associated with life. Often, they are used to stop anxiousness; maladaptive behaviors lead to non-productive and dysfunctional results in which they are more harmful than they are helpful. Maladaptive Behaviors can be grouped as dysfunctional since they give short-term assistance from discomfort and they do not cope with anxiety for a while. These behaviors are not productive as they are not doing anything0 to prevent the problem and this may serve as the strength of an underlying difficulty.

Some known maladaptive behaviors interact with panic disorder, and they include:

Avoidance

For so many people, the symptoms they get from panic disorder often provokes avoidance behavior. This can lead to agoraphobia, which is a common complication that happens in 25%-50% of people with panic disorder. Agoraphobia takes little time to unfold or can come on quickly. Some of the people suffering believe that the symptom of agoraphobia takes place immediately after their first panic attack. Immediately it takes roots; avoidance behaviors multiply quickly.

Substance Misuse

People, who have an anxiety disorder which also includes the agoraphobia and panic disorder, often use alcohol or other substance as a method of coping with anxiety and fears.

Research has shown that people who have an anxiety disorder are more likely to have substance abuse or alcohol abuse disorder than those who do not have an anxiety disorder. Abusing alcohol or other forms of drugs to control anxiety and stress is grouped as a maladaptive behavior because it provides only little relief from anxiety and this might create many more problems. Substance abuse does not fix any difficulty nor do long-term alcohol; drug abuse can lead to dependence, tolerance and for some people, addiction.

Withdrawing

Many life challenges do not need ongoing actions both mentally and behaviorally; often, we struggle and achieve success, there are also times that we struggle and yet still fail. When the latter occurs, it is possible to try again or get withdrawn from conflicts with the acceptance of our situations. When it comes to other anxiety or panic disorders, withdrawing is not attuned with recovery. This is a maladaptive behavior because it means we are going to succumb to the sickness and then not able to meet up with life's challenges. In reality, withdrawing means giving up!

Converting Anxiety to Anger

It is natural for those who are dealing with agoraphobia, panic disorder or another disorder to get frustrated easily due to their conditions. At times, this frustration leads to anger about yourself, anger towards people, and anger at what you are going through presently.

This type of anger exists in anxiety, and it's likened to a strong feeling that is natural in human experience. Everyone has felt angry at one point or another and getting angry is not exactly a bad thing. But, whenever you experience anger unhealthily, it becomes an issue with the fact that anger has a way of increasing your anxiety and makes your panic symptoms much worse. One interesting thing is that CBT works

EMOTIONAL INTELLIGENCE AND COGNITIVE BEHAVIORAL THERAPY

to manage your anger and assist you in finding ways to adapt to your anxiety.

Chapter 10: CBT for Obsession and OCD

A large database verifies the efficiency of CBT for treating OCD using E/RP. Methodologically, trials that are controlled for CBT in children and adults reported that the rate of success got to 85% (SOR: A). What qualified success, is that most of the patients responded positively to CBT, even if the symptoms remain, and there is a total cure, there might not be complete cleansing.

CBT is unlike other psychotherapies. Sadly, the total number of mental health professionals that are qualified and trained in CBT for OCD is very limited, which also includes having general information about the methods. The Obsessive-Compulsive Foundation records about 5 million Americans that have OCD lack means to behavioral therapy. Many patients that are seen in clinics have gone through traditional (talk therapies) or psychodynamics that are verified by little evidence. Such methods have the strength of recommendations (SOR) of C. As a result of this, many distressed individuals get incomplete treatment that includes medications or non-CBT psychotherapy.

Three aspects of CBT therapy for OCD

1. **Response prevention:** Preventing compulsive behaviors or ritualistic that might serve to decrease or keep away anxiety.
2. **Cognitive therapy:** Training every patient to know and avoid anxiety-provoking cognitions.
3. **Exposure:** Place the patients' circumstance that will bring about anxiety that is related to obsessions. Exposure is just for the patient to be able to confront their fears and decrease their response to anxiety.

Response Prevention

This involves you advising the patient to desist from engaging in the same continuous practices, or compulsions that are time consuming. This part is fundamentally based on the belief that rituals serve to decrease anxiety and therefore are reinforcing. Normally, E/RP is anxiety provoking for most patients, and as a result of this, it may be important to let them know that a feared circumstance will be given in an approach that is hierarchical, beginning with much easier things before moving to something harder. Once you complete the E/RP tasks guides' patient that the consequence of fears is not going to occur.

Cognitive Therapy

This takes into accounts that patients that have OCD have a different thought that is known to lead to the contribution and development and maintaining of their condition. There is a common theme that is specified within the population which includes the risk appraisal, example, "chance at which a house is burned with a cigarette is 25%."

An increased attitude for responsibility in spite of harm, example "I know the consequences of contracting HIV from using a public toilet are very slim, but I cannot be sure that I won't contract it." OCD in most adults has also been related to the way of thought-action fusion in which bad actions and thoughts are seen as synonyms. Such non-adaptive cognitive steps often make compulsive behavior, and patients with less OCD can cope with bad thoughts, the cognitive part of CBT address the issues behind it and exposes patient's ways to improve their thinking.

Exposure

Also, when the family is involved is always known to be central to the success of CBT. Family members can also help in accommodating the patients' symptoms by encouraging avoidance, inadvertently precede the growth of the disorder by taking part in rituals (example, allowing compulsive avoidance of frightened stimuli, and allow delays that are associated with completion of ritual). Taking into account,

CBT at times, gives room for the parents, patient's spouse, and other significant people.

OCD Steps

Obsessive-Compulsive Disorder brings itself in many forms, and this surely goes beyond the common misconceptions that OCD is just like a small hand wash or checking light switch. Even though, there are well-grounded OCD compulsions like perceptions that fail to acknowledge the discomforting thoughts that come before Behaviors like that which might also fail to emphasize the harm the constant compulsion can cause.

There are many types of OCD capable of improving ones thought on any issue, fear or person, and often fixes the important issues in one's life. It can improve the thought on any subject, on any fear, on any person, and often fixes what is important in someone's life. Example, if you take religion very significant, OCD fixate on random disturbing thoughts that surround religion or making the person suffering know that their thoughts or actions will offend their God. Another example given is someone who starts a new relationship, OCD makes people question their sexuality, their feelings which results in constant rumination, while the person suffering may worry that they might mislead their partners.

Though there are so many forms of OCD; it has been known that somebody's OCD will be in one of the five main steps, with themes that often extend over between the steps too.

1. Contamination/ Mental Contamination
2. Symmetry and Ordering
3. Checking
4. Hoarding
5. Ruminations/Intrusive Thoughts

Hoarding

Hoarding is also included in the list and might be an OCD compulsion if it is known for a known obsessive reason. Nevertheless, some parts of hoarding are no longer taken to be OCD and might have separate condition together; we are looking at more hoarding-related disorders.

Another form of obsession known to be included in OCD is the inefficiency to remove bad or worn out possessions, also known as 'hoarding.' Hoarding, long known to be a type of Obsessive-Compulsive Disorder was correctly reclassified in 2013 journal of DSM-5 as an uncommon condition. However, it has become complicated because there are people with Obsessive-Compulsive Disorder will hoard for particular obsessive fears or worries and can still be diagnosed with OCD instead of hoarding disorder.

Checking

There is a need to check the compulsion, but the obsessive phobia might be to remove damage, leaks, harm, or fire. Common obsessive worries and compulsions include:

- Memories
- House/office alarm
- Water taps
- Reassurance
- Gas or electric stove knobs
- Car
- Door locks and or windows
- Emails or letters
- House lights and candles
- Checking with a camera
- Electrical appliances like hair straighteners
- Driving route and checking the car
- Re-reading text

- Pregnancy
- Illness and conditions
- HIV and AIDS
- Schizophrenia
- Sexual arousal
- Valuable items like a wallet, phone, and purse.

Checking is most times carried out multiple times, sometimes hundreds of times, and this might last for an hour or even longer, causing a major effect on the person's life, work, social occasion, school, and other appointments. This can have a strong influence on a person's attitude to hold relationships and jobs, which is a reason why the phrase says 'a little bit OCD' is offensive and not accurate. Another importance of checking compulsion is that they can sometimes harm objects that are persistently being prodded, pulled, or even over tightened.

Contamination

Phobia of being dirty and contamination is worries that are obsessional, at times, fear is the contamination may cause harm to a loved one or yourself. The common compulsion might be to clean, avoid or wash, other contamination obsession worries and compulsion include:

- Eating in public locations
- Crowds
- Money
- Public toilets
- Shaking hands
- Public telephones
- GP Surgery/ Hospital
- Chemicals
- Staircase banister
- Bathroom
- Teeth brushing
- Places

- Outside air

The washing or cleaning is at times, carried out multiple times, often followed by rituals of repeating washing the body until the person knows that it is clean, instead of someone without OCD will clean or wash only once until they observe that they are clean. This can have a serious influence on the person's ability to keep relationships and jobs, and there is also a physical health impact of consistently scrubbing and cleaning on the skin, most importantly the hands. Someone might scrub until their hands bleed. While others have gone as far as bathing in bleach.

A person might also try as much as possible to keep away from places, objects, or even people if they experience fears from contaminations. There are also implications of cost due to the persistent purchase and use of cleaning products, and also of items, particularly electrical items like mobile phones that are damaged through too much liquid damage.

Mental Contamination

Additionally, there are more familiar types of OCD contaminations that involve someone washing their hands repetitively after coming in contact with potential dirty environments or objects; there is also a less known form which is called 'mental contamination.' Researchers have just started to get a basic understanding of mental contamination. The feelings of mental contamination share some important qualities with contact contamination, both having distinctive features. Feelings of mental contamination can be brought about most times when a person felt that they were treated badly, mentally, physically, via verbally or critically abusive remarks. It is sometimes as if they are meant to feel or act dirty and this creates a feeling of internal uncleanliness or even its absence of any physical contact with a harmful/dirty object. A characteristic of mental contamination is that the source is almost like that of normal human contamination which is caused by physical contact, but its own is caused by contact with inanimate objects. This might result in engaging in compulsive and repetitive attempts to clean the dirt away by washing and showering which lays the resemblance with traditional contamination OCD return; the major difference is that contaminated feeling will not need to come from physical contact, at times, there is a lonely feeling with mental contamination.

Ruminations

Ruminations is a terminology that is used to describe all obsessional intrusive thoughts, and defining rumination likely assist in encouraging the belief that "a deep or known thought about anything," but this is misleading from an OCD view. Using the context of OCD, rumination is trained to extend thinking about a theme, question that is not productive or not directed. Unlike obsessional thoughts, ruminations are just not objectionable and do not yield instead of resisting, so many ruminations are based on philosophical, metaphysical topics, religious such as life after death, the nature of morality, the origins of the universe and many more.

An example of this is when a person dwells on a time-consuming question: 'is everyone looking good?' They will also think about this for a very long period, going over it in their minds with different arguments, consideration, and contemplating compelling evidence. Another example is just someone that thinks about what will happen once they are dead, they will weigh up different possibilities theoretically, visualizing how heaven or hell might look, or other worlds, and they'll try to think about what other philosophers and scientist has discussed about death. With ruminations, it predictably never leads to a solution or satisfactory conclusion, and someone seems to be deeply rooted, thoughtful and also detached.

Preparing the Way for Your Patient

Before directing a patient for CBT, questions about the practitioner's level of training should be asked (Ph.D. or PsyD are better). Also, theoretical methods (Cognitive Behavioral vs. others, like Humanistic or Psychodynamic), and experience working with patients that have OCD should be asked. One of the questions that should be asked when meeting a clinician is "Will you allow your patients to be vulnerable to situations that bring about rituals while you are trying to refrain him or her from engaging in them?"

What Your Patients Can Expect?

CBT is a form of psychological treatment specifically based on acquiring knowledge and cognitive rules. Normally, there will be 12-16 sessions; though every individual function goes a long way in determining how long the treatment will go. The treatment can be stopped when you noticed that there is a great deal of change in the symptoms for at least four continuous weeks. Later on, timely booster sessions are useful in maintaining the benefits and prevent fallbacks.

Chapter 11: CBT for Intrusive Thoughts and OCD

Using the context of OCD, where one suffers so much from thoughts that are obsessional that is repetitive, disturbing, horrific and offensive. For example, the thought that constantly comes to you about hurting someone you love in a violent way, and this does not involve a specific compulsion, they are called intrusive thoughts, and they are often called "Pure O."

Everyone who is alive has had intrusive thoughts and of course it has been proved that everyone who has OCD will have "intrusive thoughts" which can either be positive or negative. Thinking about winning the lottery is also an intrusive thought, but it is just a great one. From the view of the OCD, it is always assumed that the thoughts are not repeating (constant) and pleasant, and it is also accepted that when you are talking about OCD 'intrusive thoughts' is of the type that will be listed below which will cover topics, but more specialization common to OCD covers the following:

Relationship Intrusive Thoughts

Relationship intrusive thoughts have preoccupied doubts that arise over how standard a relationship is; personal security of one's partner is one of the major focus for thoughts that are obsessional.

Obsessional thoughts include:

- Constantly needing to seek reassurance and the approval of one's partner.

- Doubts that a partner is faithful.

- Questioning one's sexuality, and having feelings, impulses, and thoughts about being attracted to members of the same sex.

- Constantly examining partners depth of feelings, putting the partner and the relationship under watch and always finding faults.

- The constant questioning, constant analysis of the relationship or partners often places a deep strain on the relationship and outcome when the person has OCD is that the person might break the relationship to stop anxiety and doubts which is often repeating itself with other types of relationship.

- Doubts of infidelity from another partner.

Sexual Sensitive Thoughts

Sexual sensitive thoughts are thoughts that are obsessive about causing harm that is not done purposefully. This could be thoughts of inappropriately harming children sexually. It's not intentional, or it could be a consistent thought about someone in a sexual way.

The major focus of obsessional sexual thoughts includes: is the consistent questioning of how someone can be and this are the major focus for obsessional thoughts. They include;

- The thoughts of touching a child inappropriately.

- The consistent analysis and the questioning of your sexual capability, or the thoughts about being attracted to children, are the most likely two disturbing mental parts of OCD, and because of the nature of the thoughts, many people that are suffering this are not willing to seek for assistance of any health professional and fears of being labeled.

- Fear of being attracted to people that are of the same sex (homosexuals) or fear of those who are gay, they have a fear of being attracted to people of opposite sex.

- Intrusive sexual thoughts about God, religious figures, or even about saints.

- Fear of being a pedophile and then attracted sexually to them.

Someone who experiences these types of intrusive thoughts will avoid public places like the shopping mall to keep away from getting close to children. They will also have to stay away from their siblings. For parents that experience this type of illness, they will try as much as possible to stay away from hugging or bathing their kids, which will result in emotional discomfort for both the children and the parents.

Magical Thinking about Intrusive Thoughts

Magical thinking about intrusive thoughts is having fears about thinking something negative will make it more likely for it to occur which is often referred to as 'thoughts action fusion.' The people surrounded by intrusive bad thoughts are the ones suffering, they try to take them away by going through rituals that are magical. They are conventionally strange in style and time-consuming, and they may also be involved in events or action links that may not be related to each other. Example, having the thoughts like 'I might strangle someone' is also seen as someone who is guilty of actually committing the crime. Another example is that you have terrible thoughts about your car having a ghastly accident, it might also increase the chance of it, or someone has a feeling that if they do not count 1-10 'just right' something bad might happen to a family member.

Other examples that are given below are;

- A loved one's death can be predicted.

- One can cause much harm to someone with their thoughts or carelessness.

- Attending one's funeral can bring death.

- Whatever comes to your mind can be true.

- Breaking a chain letter can bring about bad luck.

- Stepping on cracks in the pavement can allow bad things to occur.

- Hearing the word 'death' will mean the opposite like repeating the word 'life' to resist death.

- Certain days also have good or bad luck with them.

- Certain number or color has either good or bad luck that is associated with it.

In the examples above, the thoughts and events could be linked but one who has OCD will believe that the possibility of this occurring does not exist and this will lead to deep stress and anxiety. As a result of this, their internal compulsive behaviors can often keep them from interacting with other people at this time.

Religious Intrusive Thoughts

Religious intrusive thoughts with OCD are often fixed on areas of great importance, religion and matters that concern religious practice are the basic candidates for OCD obsessions. Often it is known as scrupulosity, examples of intrusive religious thoughts are listed below;

- That person has lost touch with God or their beliefs in some ways.

- Prayers are recited and omitted wrongly.

- One is doing something sinful.

- Certain prayers can be said repetitively.

- That the person has flouted religious laws that concern dress, speech, and moderations.

- Intrusive sexual thoughts about religious figures, saints, and God.

- Repeated blasphemous thoughts.

- Sins that are committed will never be forgiven by God, and one will end up in hell.

- One can have bad thoughts in a religious building.

- One will yell blasphemous words aloud in a religious location.

Intrusive bad thoughts occur during the time that prayers will be spoiled, corrupt or cancel the value of the activities, the consistent questioning, and analysis of one's faith will place a great strain on their beliefs, and this will prevent someone who derives peace from his or her religion. This will make some people avoid the church and all religious thoughts for fear of their thoughts.

Violent Intrusive Thoughts

Intrusive violent thoughts have obsessive fears of carrying out lots of violence against people you truly love or every other person. These thoughts include;

- Jumping in front of a moving car

- Thoughts about accidentally touching someone badly with the aim of touching them.

- Harming children or loved ones.

- Acting on unwanted impulse; for example, stabbing someone or running someone over.

- Poisoning the food of a loved one (compulsion will mean not cooking for the family).

- Killing innocent people

- Utilizing sharp objects such as kitchen knives.

Those suffering from this type of fear most of the time allow themselves to feel like a bad person for just having bad thoughts, they believe that having these thoughts means that they truly have the capacity of carrying it out.

The consistent questioning and analysis of this disturbing part of the OCD become more upsetting, and because of the nature of his or her thoughts, those undergoing this are reluctant to open up even to their health professional for help having a fear of being exposed. A person who has this form of intrusive thoughts will avoid places like the shopping centers and other vital areas where social interaction is required to prevent having close contacts with people that will initiate obsessional thoughts.

Body-focused Obsession (sensorimotor OCD)

Hyperawareness of the sensation of a specific body is also known to as sensorimotor obsessions. Symptoms include;

- Eye floaters/visual distractors, obsessive fixation on eye floaters

- Swallowing/salivation, focusing on how well to swallow the amount of salivation produced or sensation of swallowing itself.

- Awareness of a specific body part, example, the perception of the side of one's nose when trying to read.

- Breathing, obsessions whether you are breathing is shallow or deep, or the focus is on some other sensation of breathing.

- Blinking, obsessive fixation on blinking.

This form of OCD should not be muddled up with BDD whereby the obsession is much more about the defects that are noticed within the part of the body. The intrusive thoughts are repetitive, and they are not developed voluntarily, they make the person who suffers uncomfortable from excessive discomfort which is the reason why they are having the thoughts in the first place, and the feelings of having the thoughts in the first place can be terrifying.

However, what we know is that people are more interested in the obsessive-compulsive disorder and they might act on these thoughts, partly because they are offensive, and they can go very far from preventing it from happening.

To those suffering and those who are not suffering from it, the thoughts and the fears associated with OCD tends to be shocking and meaningful at times. Nevertheless, the fact that they are thoughts does not mean that they are developed voluntarily. Neither fantasies or impulses should be acted upon. The various information could be a physical or mental compulsion, and it does not remain helpful.

Symmetry and Orderliness

There is a need for everything that is put together in symmetric order, and 'just' right is the compulsion, the fears that are obsessive might just want you to know that everything you feel is 'just' right to stop discomfort or often prevent harm from happening. Examples include;

- Having everything spotless with no smudges on windows, on marks and surfaces less about contaminating and cleaning extra well for neatness and being right.

- Clothes.

- Arranging things neatly and at all times.

- Having your books and CD's lined up perfectly in a row on a bookshelf.

- Tinned cans.

- Having pictures well arranged.

- Having your clothes hung on rails and all facing the same way.

- Neatness.

The people that are affected spend more time trying to know the symmetry 'just right,' and this makes it more time consuming and this results in being very late to appointments and work. They can be draining both physically and mentally. If the compulsion is going to take more time, the person suffering might not want to prevent contacts at home to stop the symmetry, being interrupted and can result in having lesser impacts on social interactions and relationships.

The list shows the known common type of OCD and the fears that accompany it, but this is not a drawn list, and there will be other types of OCD. If the impacts are functioning properly, it can represent the principal part in the diagnosis of an obsessive-compulsion disorder; then it is vital for you to consult a doctor and get a proper diagnosis.

Regardless of the type of OCD one might be suffering from, the 3 following aspects are there generally, and they are; Triggers, Reassurance, and Avoidance.

1. Trigger

This is the basic source of obsessional worry which can either be a place, person, or objects that allows for obsession, a compulsive feeling, or the feelings of distress. A trigger might be internal thoughts or physical objects; for example, someone who has the obsessed feeling about stabbing someone whenever he or she comes in contact with sharp objects, seeing that the knife will always provoke the compulsions and obsessions.

Also, to avoid several hours of pain, the person will always keep away from knives, an example of an internal mental trigger is when one experiences distress obsessions about death every time the thoughts about his late father comes, the memory of their late father acts as a trigger for obsessional thoughts. What happens is that people with OCD discovered their compulsion and obsessions physically and mentally draining, scary, and frightening. They have to go to great lengths to avoiding the triggers during the time of compulsions and obsessions.

1. Avoidance

This is an occasional compulsive, and it happens where the individual with OCD keeps away from objects, places, or a person that can trigger OCD. This will be a way of preventing the anguish, distress, and the time used in undergoing the rituals. Examples include those who checks compulsion that might not be able to stay away from situations or task that will elevate the rate at which they are responsible and are not safe.

- Someone with obsessional thoughts can have the feeling of stabbing their children and will always avoid the use of scissors, knives, or any sharp objects.

- Someone who has a fear of having HIV or AIDS avoid going to places like London in which in their minds is associated with HIV or AIDS.

1. Reassurance

The person having issues with OCD will often times need reassurance that the feelings around them are not real, this reassurance can come from someone they love or through sources like the Google or news outlets. Especially if the worry is getting to the point of crimes or accidents. Frequently, the obsessional worry might be to someone you love, and you think something bad might happen to them, they will repeatedly check on their loved ones to see if they are doing fine. Another obsessional fear results in reassurance seeking for compulsive worries that their partners might not have the feeling for them or they will do something terrible to their loved one.

Various terms and acronyms can be used with the OCD family which can lead to confusions.

Acronyms commonly used for OCD

Ritual

One of the terms causing confusion is the word 'ritual' in which other people including the health professionals get confused with and then describe it as 'compulsion.' While this is certain about ritual being a compulsive behavior (mental or physical), it is just a specific compulsive behavior that is more than a set pattern of behaviors will certainly define the start and finish point. Example, massage the left side of your face, your forehead and the right side, in many cases, when the person undergoing rituals stops during the time of the ritual steps, then their OCD decides when to start their ritual over again.

Spike

Spike is also a terminology that confuses mainly those with OCD who try to get more information about it online research about it online; there tends to be two major use of this term. With people who have OCD on OCD board online; there tends to be two major use of this terms. The first one is when it is used in explaining the starting obsession 'trigger' that leads to anxiety and discomfort, example, an individual that is scared of hitting a cyclist while driving will use the term 'spike' to explain the cyclist that is moving ahead of them, and that triggers the compulsion and obsession. Another use of this term is in the OCD format is used when explaining the increase in the anxiety levels, and it is caused by obsessional thoughts. Using the example given of person that is afraid of hitting a cyclist while driving will tend to understand that the cyclist is the reason for the obsessive thoughts rising 'spike' activities.

Presently, there is no particular way to describe what spike is officially all about, but what spike means generally is that it is used to describe the joining together of OCD obsessions, triggers, or discomforts caused by anxiety which is the reasons to remove the confusions. We try as much as possible to stop using the word 'spike' in writing if there is no loss of meanings or context. So many people use terminologies to refer to different types of OCD, it is noteworthy that there is no official definition in medical science, and it is usually used by the OCD community in OCD meetings using the internet. One of the main issues with these terminologies is that they are mostly confusing since they mean something different to entirely different people. More information on the 3 major purposes on the main acronyms are;

POCD (Pedophile OCD)

This describes the postpartum and the parental OCD and 'Pure O.' Nevertheless, this is accepted widely to pedophile OCD, in few cases, we are aware of the users that use OCD consciously as a means of avoiding saying pedophile. Getting used to this line of thought is the first step in accepting that it exists. which is trying to get used to the thoughts is the first step of accepting it.

ROCD (Relationship OCD)

It is commonly used in describing the ruminating and religious OCD, which is used widely to accept mean relationship OCD because there are no medical meanings attached to it and prevent people from being confused. So, we try to stay away from acronyms whenever you are writing and make sure that you ensure that there is no loss of meaning or context. Usually, we discourage most people from trying it and on a different occasion, the use results in the delay of assessing their treatments. This mostly happens when a patient looks for a specialist in (H/P/R) OCD, but they are unable to find any since they are not recognized in medical science. There are no recommendations given yet to any specialist to specialize in any of the types of OCD since all OCD have the same way of treating the addressed C and O part.

This might not prevent progress in tackling and getting rid of OCD because it is certain that OCD that changes periodically and changes like a chameleon (note that it only focuses on objects or individuals that are special to us), as with the changes, so does the OCD. So, it is very important to treat OCD and not (H/P/R). One major point to note is that they will be treated using Cognitive Behavioral Therapy.

HOCD (Homosexual OCD)

This is not one of the helpful terminologies because it is meant for the people who are scared of being homosexual, we know that it is the same OCD that affects the homosexual with obsessional fears while they are not actually homosexual. A preferable acronym to be used is SOCD (Sexual orientation OCD)

If you are experiencing attacks frequently and you have been diagnosed with another type of anxiety disorder, it is possible to develop unintentional non-adaptive terrible methods of coping with the situation.

Treatment of OCD Intrusive Thoughts Using CBT

Those who have intrusive thoughts gotten from OCD complex PTSD intrusive thought gain from mind exercise but this usually needs treatment and self-help too. CBT has proved effective in patients (70%) with OCD. Through CBT, patients have a way of dealing with their fears and eliminate compulsions; it is an essential treatment of detoxifying the mind wholly. Modified CBT methods for treating intrusive thoughts and OCD include;

- Situational exposure
- Taking a self-report questionnaire like the OCD intrusive thoughts tests
- Gathering evidence to challenge the deep beliefs patients has

EMOTIONAL INTELLIGENCE AND COGNITIVE BEHAVIORAL THERAPY

- Role play stimulation with electronic cueing
- Intentional thought exposure
- Refocus the brain through mental education
- Deciding on the thought process each person undergoes
- Non-judgmental acceptance

Chapter 12: CBT for Mental Health and Exercise

Cognitive Tools & Exercise

Various CBT tools focus on the changing and challenging patient's dysfunctional method of thinking since CBT therapists are also taught to make use of a top-down method, first of all, working with the patient's thought, activities, and cognitive exercise are of useful importance. To change the downward spiral or reverse mental health disorder, patients will know about the cognitive restructuring and begin to use tools like the dysfunctional thought records and the ABCD strategies.

Behavioral Tools & Exercise

Besides the cognitive tools and exercise, CBT therapist teaches their client's various behavioral methods that might help change the problematic thoughts and limiting beliefs into life-affirming alternatives. By taking a strong action that is against what they may tell themselves, individuals are more able to compile the evidence that goes against harming cognitive patterns. Very good examples of behavioral tools are behavioral experiments, behavioral rehearsal, and behavioral activation.

Tools from Third-Wave Therapies

There are additional ways of various means of innovative third wave therapeutic methods that are gotten from CBT, and this provides new additions to the CBT toolbox. While not all the therapist use what is known to be considered to be a third-wave activities or exercise, it is of note to them because it can help achieve dreams, specific tools that are found in the third-wave therapies like the Acceptance and Commitment Therapy (ACT) and Mindfulness-Based Cognitive therapy (MBCT) is very useful for our endeavors.

Mental Health Ailments that may improve with CBT

Handle grief

The client and therapist additionally consider how thoughts and behaviors affect emotions. For instance, if someone thinks that nothing could work out to them in life, they can withdraw from others and also prevent brand new chances. This, subsequently, can lead to feelings of increased despair, emptiness, and stress. This is sometimes known as a "vicious circle" of emotions, thoughts, and behaviors.

Try to be patient: Even though CBT performs fast for lots of individuals, it's an ongoing procedure that's essentially life-long. There are always approaches to boost, feel happier, and also treat others and yourself better, so exercise being individual. Remind yourself there is no finish line. Give your self-credit for placing effort into confronting your issues immediately, and attempt and look at "slip ups" as certain parts of the process and mastering procedure.

PTSD

CBT is most commonly applied to mood disorders (for example, depression) and anxiety disorders. It is likewise used to aid individuals who have chemical use complications, personality disorders, eating disorders, sexual issues, and psychosis. It is properly delivered into the personal, couples, and group formats.

A psychotherapist can be an overall period, instead of a job title or hint of education, instruction or licensure. Examples of psychotherapists consist of psychiatrists, psychologists, certified professional counselors, licensed social workers, certified marriage and family therapists, psychiatric nurses, or even other certified practitioners with mental wellness coaching.

Your therapist may persuade you to discuss your thinking and emotions and what's troubling you. Do not be concerned if you simply still discover that it's tough to open about your feelings. Your therapist will assist you to gain greater confidence and comfort.

The Downward Spiral of Mental Disorder

A mother and daughter crying with their heads bowed down, it looks like a tragic event took place in their lives leading to a downward spiral towards negative mental health disorder. The CBT therapist can give their patients good treatment methods on an individual basis. This, however, does not mean that mental illness brings themselves in separate ways; there is much disorder that is being influenced by genes or life experiences that develops closely in a systematic approach.

For those who are suffering from depression or anxiety; an example, bad events or set of successful order typically set of successful events typically leads to the beginning of cognitive behavioral and emotional symptoms, especially when an individual cannot stop or reverse their anxiousness or depressive response they will start spiraling downwards towards a full mental disorder.

The CBT examined previously to assist in showing the downward spiral mental health disorders because it shows us how the problematic thoughts, emotional response, behaviors, and emotional response can respectively influence another by needing medical assistance. The damaged cognitive ways of an individual who loses a premature loved one, example, this can be of negative influence as their behaviors and emotions are ways that lead to a serious depressive disorder.

Certainly, grieving the loss of someone you love can be healthy to some extent but if the individual affected is unable to break the cycle of cognitions, behaviors, and emotions negatively affecting one another, they will be spiral downward to a state of fear. To assist them from a depressive state, a CBT therapist will represent various cognitive behavioral activities that are the opposite direction of the downward spiral.

It should be known that CBT therapist first works with the parent's level behavior and cognition, they will often have to assist them in discovering the change core value, challenge and underlying assumptions of how the world will move them in the direction of stabilized mental health.

Chapter 13: CBT for Self-Monitoring & Progress Evaluation

Two most essential CBT methods are the practices of self-monitoring and examining progress, by raising self-awareness and most times assess the state of one's being, individuals are also able to discover the faulty cognitions, limiting the core values, patterns of dysfunctional thinking, and behavioral hindrances. With this powerful insight, CBT therapist will guide the parents in taking steps that will prevail whether a behavior or mental obstacle.

The practices of self-monitoring and evaluation are the heart of CBT, just as every individual can prevail over mental illness by becoming conscious of the challenging behaviors and improving the probability for success by enhancing and monitoring the actions and thoughts. Great practices that can widely increase the awareness of the inhibiting thoughts, harmful behaviors and limiting beliefs that act as roadblocks on the path of success is the third strategy of mindful meditation.

While undertaking practices of SMART goals, self-monitoring, action plans, and self-evaluation, it is typically enough to make individuals achieve success and decrease the amount of time it takes to achieve goals by using several CBT tools. Basing decisions on and attaching to general psychological governing principles like the mind-body connection and the law of effects and cause, just as the CBT practitioners assist their patients to do, we can confidently transform our lives in the most necessary ways. After we begin to spin the positive spiral of personal growth with the CBT methods, the following will be used to build our starting momentum.

The CBT Toolbox

There are a wide variety of CBT tools that therapist use to improve the mental health of their patients, unlike some treatment methods, cognitive behaviors therapy helps to limit the way parents rely on the medications rather than focusing on establishing a behavioral and cognitive change through various modes of exercise and activities. After establishing a case formulation gotten from initial therapeutic communications with their patients, a CBT therapist will start recommending several cognitive and behavioral practices that are found within the toolbox of CBT. The exercise from the toolbox is vital due to the long-term necessity to give patients the resources to act as their therapist later in the future.

While there are several activities and exercises that may be used for a specific medical case, or favored by a particular therapist, there is an accepted range set for CBT methods based on their effectiveness and popularity. It is with standardized tools and techniques that can be used to enhance the success of achieving our aim or goals. We will examine, but it will be useful to gain more understanding of how CBT therapists frame their treatments methods.

Using CBT to Achieve Success

Since the basis of CBT is upon several psychological truths that are applied to everyone, they all can use the CBT methods to improve our level of wellbeing. Also, a CBT therapist assists their patients to change their downward spiral mental health; it is possible to use CBT tools as a springboard to success. One ideological way to meditate on using CBT for personal growth is to envision a scale that ranges from -5 to 0, represent every individual who has mental illness while the range of 0 to 5 represents healthy minded individuals that pursue high levels of life satisfaction. It is obvious to note that implementing CBT methods to improve your self-worth, you will learn fast on how positive emotions and thoughts can spiral you towards great success.

Defining Success

While there is an endless number of a personal growth goal that you can use CBT methods to achieve, the first step is to know which one will guarantee you success. Unfortunately, many people fall victim to assuming that materials, money, possessions, and social status will give them the satisfaction that is needed only to discover that limited happiness is achieved from them.

SMART Goals & Action Plan

The therapist and clients work together to establish a SMART goal that is (Specific, Measurable, Achievable, Relevant & Time-Bound) and make an achievable plan that assists towards accomplishing their desire. Typically, both the patient and therapist will meet together on a scheduled basis to review, update the client's formulations, goals, and action plan.

We know what success is all about, we can establish the SMART goals. Generally, we may consider having goals in a number of the following steps; Personal & Intellectual, Health Fitness, Spiritual, Financial & Professional Developments and Communication. Also, personal qualities like social intelligence and emotional may be difficult to measure; these are some of the most vital and rewarding goals to help because they are needed to achieve some extraordinary things. Just by committing yourself to also focusing on targets that are intrinsic and desires, in addition to this external success, you will be able to discover the life-satisfaction that is craved for. Before moving to the action plan, you need to consider your objectives using SMART goals. There is no reason to feel discouraged if you have the aim to achieve something monumental, you will have to put the bigger aspirations down into smaller, time-bound and measurable. You will have to reduce the bigger goals into smaller, time-bound and measurable goals.

The next step in using the process of CBT for success, which is to be considered the final step in the initial phase, would be to establish a management plan that might allow you to monitor your progress. While deciding on the methods that will be used to break down specific objectives will be for a particular individual option that is mainly based on situations and plans, the most necessary thing to do is to review and update your appropriate measurable and time-bound action plan.

Chapter 14: How CBT Deals With Things

There are just so many methods of achieving CBT or tools that can be used in CBT. This therapy extends from the background of the therapy to daily life experiences. The nine methods have been listed below, and some are known to be an effective and common practice of CBT.

- Unraveling Cognitive Distortions

This one of the main aim of Cognitive Behavioral Therapy and this can be done without or with the aid of a therapist, just to unfold the hold of the Cognitive aberrations, first be conscious of the aberrations that you are most likely to be exposed to, part of which involves you must be able to identify and challenge our injurious automatic thoughts, which from time to time fall into any categories listed beforehand.

This is one of the main aims of Cognitive Behavioral Therapy and it can be done without or with the aid of a therapist. To unravel cognitive distortions, you must first be conscious of the distortions you may likely be exposed to. It also involves you identifying and challenging those negative thoughts that pop up in our minds from time to time.

- Exposure and Response Prevention

This kind of method is specifically effective for people that undergo hardship of obsessive-compulsive disorder (OCD), you must be able to practice this type of method by being vulnerable to whatever evokes a compulsive behavior, but also do your best to hold back from writing about it and the behavior. It is possible to add together journaling with these methods to get how this method can make you feel.

- Journaling

This method is a means of "collecting data" concerning our thoughts and moods, this journal must contain the period of the mood or thought, it's the source, the range or the degree of strength among so many other things. This necessary CBT tools and methods can assist us in learning our emotional tendencies and thoughts, find out how they are replaced, how they adapt, or the way at which they are able to cope with it.

- Cognitive Restructuring

Immediately, you have been able to know exactly what the aberrations are or the views that are not accurate, you then start to understand how the aberrations started and what exactly made you believe in it. When you know that it is a behavior that is harmful or injurious, you can start to confront it. Example, when you have the consciousness that you have a job that pays well and earns you respect within the society, but then you lost paying job, you will start to feel terrible about yourself. Rather than accepting this belief that makes you think bad about yourself, you can think about the occasion that allows you feel like a well know respectable person, a belief that may not have come to your mind before.

- Nightmare Exposure and Rescripting

Nightmare vulnerability and rescripting are designed specifically to those who are going through difficult moments of a nightmare; this method is also known to be almost the same as interceptive exposure, in that the nightmare has been evoked which then bring up emotions. The therapist and the client must work together to know what type of emotions are desired and how to develop new images to follow the emotions that are desired.

- Progressive Muscle Relaxation

This is a known method to those that practice being mindful, also the same as the body scan; this method will teach you how to relax a type of your muscle group at a period whereby your body falls under the state of necessary CBT methods and relaxation tools. It's possible to use a YouTube video, audio guidance, or just using your mind to know how to practice these methods and this can be most helpful for calming nerves and soothing an unfocused and busy mind.

- Introspective Exposure

This method is designed to treat anxiety and panic; it includes being exposed to bodily excitement that is feared in order to evoke responses activating unhealthy beliefs that are known to be connected with the excitements, preserve the sensations without avoiding them or distraction and this allows acquiring new things about the sensations. It is designed to help the person suffering to understand that the symptoms of this panic are not harmful, though, it can be very uncomfortable.

- Play the script until the End

This method is basically for those that are undergoing anxiety and fears, using this type of method, the individual that is exposed to crippling anxiety or fears controls experimental thoughts where they are able to think about the result of the worst-case models. Allowing this scenario to assist the client to know that even when it seems, there will be fears, it will turn out very good. This method will assist those with anxiety and fears to believe that their worst fears would eventually turn out to be good experience.

- Relaxed Breathing

This is another method which is not known to CBT but is very popular among the mindful practitioners; there are many obvious ways to relax and also bring orderliness and calmness to your breathing, which gives you an edge to see your problems from a balanced position, bringing about more efficient and logical decision-making. These methods can assist those who are going through a range of mental afflictions and illness which includes OCD, depression, panic disorder, anxiety and how they can be practiced without or with the aid of a therapist.

Getting the Most out of it

CBT can be applied daily to principles and methods that surround a wide range of problems. Relaxation skills are very much essential in any stressful circumstance which includes; speaking in public, having an argument with partners, feeling angry at a stubborn teenager, taking a test, sleep problems, and road rage.

Problem-solving methods can be useful in dealing with related issues that concern work that is prioritizing, a demanding boss and time management or interpersonal difficulties or relationship problems. Some people have some attitudes that are irrational, and this creates unnecessary bad feelings in certain situations.

So, anyone can also gain from disputing and identifying unfounded beliefs and this result in experiences that have less bad emotions, and this can be more effective in their lives. Exposure exercise is not just helpful in phobias but as a way of removing all types of fears which include fears of making mistakes, fears of animals, and fear of heights. Additionally, CBT techniques are more useful to every one of our lives whether they have a psychological disorder or those who deal with real-life solutions.

Chapter 15: Final Thoughts on Cognitive Behavioral Therapy

CBT was initially created to assist people afflicted by depression; however today it is utilized to boost and control different types of emotional illnesses and symptoms, for example, anxiety, bipolar illness, post-traumatic stress illness, obsessive-compulsive disease, addictions, and eating disorders.

CBT techniques will also be favorable to just about everybody, for example, people with no type of emotional disease but with chronic anxiety, inferior moods, and habits they want to do their job with.

Scientific tests have discovered that in most those who have accomplished CBT and then undergone brain scans proves that CBT is capable of favorably adjusting physical structures inside mental performance.

CBT can get the job done fast, assisting people to feel better and experience lessened symptoms within a quick period (a few months, for instance).

When many kinds of therapy could take some months or even years to become beneficial, the average quantity of CBT periods clients receive is 16.

CBT often requires the individual finishing "homework" duties independently amongst therapy sessions, which is one reason benefits come so fast.

In addition to prep being done from the people while they truly are alone, cognitive behavioral therapists also utilize instructions, such as coughing and "vulnerability therapy" throughout periods.

CBT is extremely interactive and collaborative. The therapist's role would always be there to listen, teach and encourage, while the individual's role is to be more open and expressive.

What Next For the Future of CBT?

Several strategies and benefit of CBT have been discussed so far in this book. Here is a recap and some closing thoughts about CBT and reasons why it may be best for you.

The evolution of cultural adaptations into CBT is still at the beginning phases. CBT hinges predominantly on the values supported from the dominant civilization. Back in North America, these values incorporate assertiveness, personal independence, verbal power, logic and behavior change. But specific manuals are created for adapting CBT to Chinese-Americans and Haitian-American adolescents.

Cognitive behavioral therapy (CBT) can be just a usual sort of conversation therapy (psychotherapy). You work with a mental wellness counselor (psychotherapist or therapist) in a structured manner, attending quite a limited amount of sessions. CBT makes it possible to become aware of wrong or unwanted thoughts, and that means you can view challenging scenarios more certainly and respond in your mind in a better way.

In CBT, the therapist and the customer come together to determine unhelpful patterns of thinking and behavior. By way of instance, somebody might just notice the bad things that happen to these and never notice the positive things. Or, someone could put unrealistic specifications on their own, such as "creating blunders in the office is improper." Also, it is essential to determine curable behaviors that take outward symptoms, such as avoiding particular situations and withdrawing from others.

It is crucial that you decide to try and view predicaments as rationally, clearly and realistically as you possibly can. It is helpful to think about different people's perspectives, question your premises, and see whether there is something crucial you may be missing or dismissing.

How Many CBT Sessions Will You Need to Get the Desired Result?

CBT is commonly regarded as short-term therapy—approximately 10 to 20 sessions. You along with your therapist can talk about how many sessions may be appropriate for you personally.

At your first session, your therapist will collect information on you personally and get exactly what concerns you may have. The therapist will likely inquire regarding your present and past physical and emotional health to gain a deeper comprehension of your circumstance. Your therapist can discuss if you might benefit from additional treatment as well, like medication.

The therapist works together with clients to tackle unfavorable perspectives the consumer retains about itself, the world and the future, which may bring about feelings of despair.

Is CBT limited in Any Way?

CBT doesn't have limitations because it can be adapted to solve various issues. Carefully assembled exercises are used to support and modify feelings and behaviors. Some therapies focus more on notions, and also some aspects focus a lot more on behaviors. When someone has trouble identifying and challenging mental issues, the therapist might focus on addressing behaviors like avoidance, withdrawal, or poor interpersonal knowledge.

On the other hand, if this sort of behaviors is less noticeable, the therapist may focus on low-self-esteem.

The very first session is also an opportunity for you to interview your therapist to find out whether he or she's going to be a good fit for you personally.

Learning About Your Emotional Health Condition

Recognize troubling situations or illnesses in your life is part of therapy. These may include problems such as a medical condition, divorce, despair, anger or symptoms of mental illness. You and your therapist may dedicate some time to identify the problems and aims that you want to focus on. Cognitive behavioral therapy may be achieved one-on-one, or even in categories together with family members with those that have similar difficulties.

What You May Anticipate

CBT typically specializes in special issues, utilizing a goal-oriented strategy. Since you proceed through the therapy approach, your therapist might ask you to do "assignments"—tasks, examining through or practices that build on what you find out during your regular therapy sessions—and invite you to utilize exactly what you are learning into your normal lifestyle.

Identify Strategies to Manage Emotions

Cognitive behavioral therapy can be utilized to take care of a vast variety of issues. It is usually the preferred kind of psychotherapy as it could quickly help you determine and cope with challenges that are specific. It usually requires fewer periods than different forms of therapy and can be done in a coordinated way.

Ways to Practice Cognitive Behavioral Therapy Techniques on Your Own

1. Describe your present obstacles

The very first thing to do is to identify what's causing you to worry, unhappiness and unease. Maybe you're feeling resentful toward someone, fearful of failure, or stressed about being refused socially in some way. You might realize that you have persistent stress, indicators of melancholy, or are fighting to forgive somebody for a past event. When you can recognize this and become aware of your main barrier, then you have the power to start work on overcoming it.

1. Be wary of your emotions, thoughts, and beliefs about these issues.

When you have determined the issues to focus on, your therapist will encourage you to discuss your thinking regarding these. This could consist of celebrating what you know about experience, your perspective of a situation, and your self-beliefs, other people and events. Your therapist will recommend you keep a journal of your thoughts.

1. Be able to look after yourself securely

Reshape incorrect or negative thinking. Your therapist will likely encourage you to inquire if an opinion of a situation is situated in fact or in an erroneous perception of what's going on. This step might be difficult. You may have long-standing ways of thinking in your own life as well as yourself. Together with exercise, very beneficial thinking, and behavior styles will grow to be a custom and will not take as much work.

1. Evaluate your queries

Previous to your very first consultation, consider what issues you want to work on while you can also sort out this along with your therapist, even having a few senses beforehand can give a starting point.

EMOTIONAL INTELLIGENCE AND COGNITIVE BEHAVIORAL THERAPY

1. Cope with a medical issue

Even though CBT has been used with kids as young as seven to nine years older, it is most effective with kids with the age of fourteen years. At this age, kids have significantly more improved cognitive skills. Younger kids, or teens and adults, who have cognitive disabilities, generally reply to behavioral plans and ridding of the environment as opposed to a focus on believing.

Make Sure That You know:

- The severity of your outward symptoms
- Identifying scenarios which are frequently averted and steadily approaching dreaded situations
- Popular CBT interventions
- Sexual ailments
- The length of every session

Generally, there is a minimal threat in receiving cognitive behavioral therapy. Because it might research debilitating feelings, emotions, and adventures, you can feel mentally uncomfortable at times. You will shout, be angry or truly feel upset during a session that is tough, or you could even feel drained. You may also threaten to instantly or soon (imminently) hurt yourself or take your own life.

The therapist and client work with each other to anticipate problems and develop successful working strategies. Differentiating and challenging negative thoughts (e.g., "Things never work outside for me personally").

Do your assignments among sessions. If a therapist asks you to browse, maintain a diary, or perform alternative activities outside of your routine therapy sessions to check along with. Doing these homework assignments will allow you to apply what you have learned from the therapy periods.

Stick to your treatment program. In the event you truly feel down or lack motivation, it can be tempting to skip therapy sessions. Doing so can interrupt your progress. Enroll in all sessions and offer a notion about exactly which you want to focus on.

Identifying and engaging in enjoyable activities including hobbies, social pursuits, and physical exercise.

You can apply cognitive behavioral therapy by pinpointing your current challenges, stressful thought recording, forming patterns, and understanding your triggers, discovering how matters are constantly shifting, placing yourself in others' shoes, and thanking yourself for being patient.

One of the primary advantages of patients is that CBT can be continued even after formal sessions with a therapist are over.

Generally, there are few risks in getting CBT. However, you may experience uncomfortable situations at times as it can explore emotions, bad feelings and experiences which may cause you to cry or feel upset during the CBT session. All these are steps and processes to overcome your challenge and develop better coping skills.

Finally, after proper therapy ends, the person could carry on working on researching CBT concepts, applying techniques they've figured out, reading and journaling to aid in lengthening gains and taking care of signs or symptoms.

Conclusion

CBT is a practical therapy to deal with emotional challenges. Various kinds of CBT, like exposure therapy, might ask that you confront predicaments you would rather avert—such as flying in airplanes when you harbor a fear of traveling. This also can result in temporary pressure or anxiety. The impact of CBT therapy in solving most of the disorders and mental issues mentioned in this book cannot be overemphasized as it has been proven to be more effective than other similar therapies.

CBT techniques may also be beneficial for just about everybody, for example, people without a kind of mental disease but who have chronic pressure, poor moods and habits they'd like to work with.

Be honest and open as success with this therapy is dependent on your willingness to share your thoughts, emotions, and experiences, and on being open to fresh insights and means of doing matters. If you're reluctant to discuss certain issues due to debilitating emotions, embarrassment or fears regarding your therapist's response, then allow your therapist to understand regarding your bookings.

CBT isn't the best way for all clients. Those who have significantly more chronic or recurring illness may need repeated interventions. Or they could need a change to tactics apart from CBT to tackle early life adventures along with personal, interpersonal, and identity troubles. And given that CBT can be quite a valuable device in treating emotional health disorders, including depression, post-traumatic stress disorder (PTSD) or an eating disorder. However, perhaps not everybody who benefits from CBT comes with a mental health state. It can be effective tools to assist anyone who learns how to manage difficult daily living conditions.

Before seeing a psychotherapist, check his or her approaches for handling and preventing risky scenarios. You may decide in your mind that you wish to try cognitive behavioral therapy. Or just a health care provider or somebody else may indicate therapy to you. Do not expect instant outcomes. Working on emotional issues can be debilitating and usually requires hard work. It's not unusual to feel worse throughout the initial portion of therapy as you start to confront past and current battles. You may require several sessions before you begin to observe advancement.

This book has touched on every essential aspect of CBT and how to improve your lives and those around you who may be suffering from any emotional challenge. List of cognitive behavioral therapy methods is far from being exhaustible, but this will give you other good ideas on the different methods that are used during cognitive behavioral therapy when working with a therapist and you have been doing your reading about CBT, then you can tell your therapist what type of methods excite you.

I hope you will find strength as you begin to use these therapies to your advantage. I hope it works perfectly for you or other people you recommend it to. I would love to hear your success story after using the steps highlighted in this book.

© Copyright 2019 - All rights reserved.

The content contained within this book may not be reproduced, duplicated or transmitted without direct written permission from the author or the publisher.

Under no circumstances will any blame or legal responsibility be held against the publisher, or author, for any damages, reparation, or monetary loss due to the information contained within this book. Either directly or indirectly.

Legal Notice:

This book is copyright protected. This book is only for personal use. You cannot amend, distribute, sell, use, quote or paraphrase any part, or the content within this book, without the consent of the author or publisher.

Disclaimer Notice:

Please note the information contained within this document is for educational and entertainment purposes only. All effort has been executed to present accurate, up to date, and reliable, complete information. No warranties of any kind are declared or implied. Readers acknowledge that the author is not engaging in the rendering of legal, financial, medical or professional advice. The content within this book has been derived from various sources. Please consult a licensed professional before attempting any techniques outlined in this book.

By reading this document, the reader agrees that under no circumstances is the author responsible for any losses, direct or indirect, which are incurred as a result of the use of information contained within this document, including, but not limited to, — errors, omissions, or inaccuracies.

www.ingramcontent.com/pod-product-compliance
Lightning Source LLC
LaVergne TN
LVHW041944070526
838199LV00051BA/2896